SUCH A NUISANCE TO DIE

SUCH A NUISANCE TO DIE

The Autobiography of Her Serene Highness
Princess Elisabeth de Croÿ,
A Royal Ambassador for Animals

Elisabeth de Croÿ
as told to Joy Leney

Book Guild Publishing
Sussex, England

First published in Great Britain in 2010 by
The Book Guild Ltd
Pavilion View
19 New Road
Brighton, BN1 1UF

Typesetting in Garamond by
Keyboard Services, Luton, Bedfordshire

Printed and bound in Great Britain by
CPI Antony Rowe

A catalogue record for this book is available from
The British Library

ISBN 978 1 84624 448 3

'It is such a nuisance to die when there is so much more I need to do to help people and animals'

Elisabeth de Croÿ-Solre, 1921–2009

Coat of Arms: Des Ancien Rois de Hongrie

Credit: Nobiliaire d'Austrasie, Tome 1. De Croÿ, Des Anciens Rois de Hongrie

This book is dedicated to Dylan, Poppy, Grace, Luca and Santana and all young people everywhere. Spread your wings, travel, explore new horizons, live a full and active life, but remember to do something useful to help fellow humans and all other creatures that share your world.

Château d'Azy, built 1846, the family home of Elisabeth

Contents

Photographs and Credits

Cover photo: 1964. Elisabeth and Gri Gri, a rescue dog. *Credit: RdeT collection.*

Coat of Arms: Des Ancien Rois de Hongrie. *Credit: Nobiliaire d'Austrasie, Tome 1. De Croÿ, Des Anciens Rois de Hongrie*

Château d'Azy, built 1846, the family home of Elisabeth. *Credit: Jon Bradley.*

p. xxiii. Photo of Jenny Seagrove. *Credit: Gill Shaw.*

Introduction: Elisabeth the Activist

p. xxxiv. Elisabeth at home. *Credit: RdeT collection.*

p. xxxiv. 1997. Chu-nan, Taiwan. Government dog pound, cages on a garbage site where dogs were left to starve to death. *Credit: WSPA/LCA.*

p. xxxv. 1997. Elisabeth in a cage on a garbage site at Chu-nan removing the catching wires from dogs that had been left to starve to death. *Credit: WSPA/LCA.*

p. xxxv. 1997. A private dog shelter in Taiwan where we took the dogs rescued from the Chu-nan government dog pound. *Credit: WSPA/LCA.*

Chapter 1 Brief Overview of Family Background

p. 4. Château de Bellignies, Belgium. The family home of Prince Léopold, Princess Marie and Prince Reginald. The tower on the left which dates from the Middle Ages, contains the hidden staircase. Photo taken after restoration following the war. *Credit: J Mercier-Hautmont (Nord).*

p. 5. c.1960. Prince Léopold, Princess Marie, Prince Reginald in later life. *Credit: Family collection.*

p. 12. 1934. Prince Léopold de Croÿ-Solre, my father. *Credit: Family collection.*

p. 13. c.1925. Princess Jacqueline, my mother. *Credit: Family collection.*

p. 14. 1922. Me, aged 1 month with my parents Princess Jacqueline and Prince Léopold. *Credit: Family collection.*

p.15. 1925. Nurse Henderson, my wonderful nurse. *Credit: Family collection.*

p. 17. c.1932. On holiday with my sisters, brother and nanny (me, 5th from left). *Credit: Family collection.*

p. 18. 1932. My sister Marie Dorothée and me (right) with our maternal grandmother, the Marquise de Lespinay. *Credit: Family collection.*

p. 19. c.1937. Me with Miniska. *Credit: Novaphot. 4. Rue du 14 Juillet, Nevers.*

p. 20. c.1945.My sisters, left to right: Princesses Claire, Marie Dorothée, Catherine, Florence, Jacqueline-Rose, Emmanuela. *Credit: Studio de France, 3. Rue du Colisée, Paris. Ely 17–96.*

Chapter 2 Spreading My Wings

p. 28. 1994. Chair from the music room used by Chopin at the home of my great-grandmother – now used by animals at my home! *Credit RdeT collection.*

p. 29. c.1950. As President of the Debutante Ball getting ready for the Ball at Versailles. *Credit: Charles of the Ritz, 51 Av Montalgne, Paris – V111*

p. 30. 1950. Preparing for the Debutantes ball at the Palace of Versailles. *Credit: Louis Peltier, actualities Eclair Continental, 38 rue Victor-Basch 33, Montrouge.*

p. 32. c.1960s. Wearing a cat mask at an Embassy party in Paris. *Credit: Y M Pech, 322 Rue Saint Jacques, 322 Paris-V.*

p. 33. c.1950. On a skiing holiday at St Anton, Austria. *Credit: Foto Rio St Anton am Ariberg.*

p. 34. c. 1952.With friends on the beach in the Bahamas. *Credit: Vega Keane.*

p. 36. c.1950. Party girl! *Credit: RdeT collection.*

p. 37. c.1953. Wearing a fur coat before I knew better! *Credit: Eddy van der veen, Rue Choron, Paris.*

p. 39. c.1960s. Reception at the Belgian Embassy, Paris. Ex-Queen Marie-Jose of Italy (left) speaking with me and an Embassy official. *Credit: R. Delhay, 30 Avenue Aristide-Briand 30, Stains (Seine) Paris.*

p. 40. 1962. Reception at the Belgian Embassy, Paris. Queen Elisabeth of Belgium (left) me (centre). *Credit: Photographiques International, Agence L.A.P.I. Les Actualities, R. Delhay Director Bureau, 9, Cour Petites Ecuries, Paris-X.*

p. 41. c.1960s. Reception at the Belgian Embassy in Paris. L to R: Baroness Yolaine de Candé; Baroness Jaspar and me. *Credit: R. Delhay, 30 Avenue Aristide-Briand 30, Stains (Seine) Paris.*

p. 42. 1964. Executive Committee of the First World Festival of African Art. Left to right: President Léopold Senghor of Senegal, Duchess of Rochefoucauld, me (President of the Committee), André Malraux, Minister of Culture. *Credit: Photo by J. Campbell.*

Chapter 3 The Lure of America

p. 51. 1964. Duchess of Windsor with TV Presenter Léon Zitrone (left) at the Christmas Party for Animals in Paris. *Credit: Paris-Jour/Michel Hermans.*

p. 52. 1965. At the home of the Duchess of Windsor, Paris, to organise the Christmas Party for Animals. *Credit: Paris-Jour/Michel Hermans.*

p. 53. 1972. Christmas Party for Animals. Left to right: Dr Méry (Founder of CNPA), SPA official; me, Mme Messmer (wife of the Prime Minister). *Credit: Photo Patrice Picot. Jours de France.*

p. 55. 1962. At la Belle et la Bête charity dog show. *Credit: Apis-Paris 43 Rue de Trevise. Photo Daniel Conde.*

p. 56. 1961. We win 1st prize at la Belle et la Bête charity dog show. *Credit: R. Dehesdin. Studios Vendome-Flash, 12 Place Vendome, Paris.*

p. 58. 1961. Showing the 1st prize trophy to Marquis. *Credit: RdeT collection.*

p. 59. 1962. Leaving Paris for New York to attend the 'April in Paris' Charity Ball at the Hotel Pierre. *Credit: Pan American World Airways Overseas Division. NY. International Airport.*

p. 61. 1962. A sign in Times Square, New York, USA to welcome me! *Credit: RdeT collection.*

p. 62. 1962. President John F. Kennedy, 35th President of the United States of America at The White House, Washington DC, USA. *Credit: RdeT collection.*

p. 65. 1965. Lima, Peru. Helping at the zoo clinic with Carmen Benavides. *Credit: RdeT collection.*

p. 66. 1965. Lima, Peru. With Carmen Benavides at the clinic, cleaning the dog's wounds. *Credit: RdeT collection.*

p. 67. 1965. Lima, Peru. An emaciated horse, sadly not an unusual sight. *Credit: H.R. Ramus, Fotographia commercial, Nicloas de Pierola 1014, Lima, Peru.*

Chapter 4 Life Changing Events

p. 72. c.1929. St Benin d'Azy, getting ready for the Boar Hunt. *Credit: Family collection.*

p. 74. 1956. Algeria. Having tea with French allies during the war in Algeria. *Credit: RdeT collection.*

p. 74. 1956. Algeria. A temporary resting place during the war in Algeria. *Credit: RdeT collection.*

p. 75. 1956. Algeria. During field training in preparation for any surprise attacks. *Credit: RdeT collection.*

p. 89. 1969. Biafra, Nigeria. A typical scene of starving children, the innocent victims of the war. *Credit: Comité d'Action Pour le Biafra, 18 Avenue de Friedland 18 75-PARIS.*

p. 90. 1969. Biafra, Nigeria. Elisabeth with Madame Nijoleka Ojukwu, wife of General Ojukwu. *Credit: Comité d'Action Pour le Biafra, 18 Avenue de Friedland 18 75-PARIS.*

Chapter 5 Road to the Refuge

p. 102. 1933. Letter from my father to me on my 12th birthday. *Credit: RdeT collection.*

p. 103. 1933. Letter from my father to me on my 12th birthday. *Credit: RdeT collection.*

p. 105. c.1960. With my dear Aunt Marie, Princess Marie de Croÿ-Solre. *Credit: RdeT collection.*

p. 108. 1969. Early days at *Refuge de Thiernay. Credit: Gérard Bidolet, 7. Place du Champ de Foire 58 Decize.*

p. 109. 1969. Early days at *Refuge de Thiernay. Credit: Gérard Bidolet, 7. Place du Champ de Foire 58 Decize.*

p. 110. 1970. George de Caunes, TV star and animal lover cutting the ribbon at the Opening of *Refuge de Thiernay. Credit: RdeT collection.*

p. 111. 1987. At Wood Green Animal Shelters, Cambridgeshire with Graham Fuller, Chief Executive Officer. *Credit: WGAS.*

p. 112. 1994. Entrance to *Refuge de Thiernay. Credit: RdeT collection.*

p. 112. 1994. Typical dog enclosure at *Refuge de Thiernay. Credit: RdeT collection.*

p. 113. 1994. Typical cat enclosure at *Refuge de Thiernay. Credit: RdeT collection.*

p. 113. 1997. Animal Behaviour training session at *Refuge de Thiernay* with Dr Roger Mugford. *Credit RdeT collection.*

p. 116. 1996. David Griffiths demonstrating a spay operation at the *Refuge de Thiernay* neutering week 1996. *Credit: RdeT collection.*

p. 116. 1997. Education week at *Refuge de Thiernay.* Left to right: Dr. Pawel Novak (Poland), Kate Fernald (veterinary student from USA), Pei-Feng Su (Taiwan). *Credit: RdeT collection.*

p. 117. 2000. Josiane Cœuret, Secretary General of *Refuge de Thiernay* and my 'right-hand-woman'. *Credit: RdeT collection.*

Chapter 6 Dance, Seals and Traps

p. 124. 1957. The beautiful ballerina Lilavati. *Credit: RdeT collection.*

p. 127. 1988. Prince Edward Island, Canada with a beautiful baby seal. *Credit: Mary Bloom/IFAW.*

p. 128. 1988. With Trap-trap, a stray dog badly injured when caught in a leg-hold trap. *Credit: RdeT collection.*

p. 129. 1988. European Parliament, Strasbourg showing the leg-hold traps to Eileen Lemass, the MEP for Ireland. *Credit: Eurogroup for Animal Welfare.*

p. 130. 1988. At the European Parliament, Strasbourg discussing leg-hold traps with (left to right) Lord Plum, President of the European

Parliament; Ian Ferguson, Director of Eurogroup. *Credit: Eurogroup for Animals.*

Chapter 7 Missions in Eastern Europe

p. 134. 2003. Campaigning with Naturewatch UK in Kiev. *Credit: Naturewatch.*
p. 136. 1989. Arriving at a monastery in Poland with donated supplies from France. *Credit: Jenny Remfry.*
p. 137. 1989. Jenny Remfry (right) with the Manager of the Wroclaw branch of TOZ. *Credit: Jenny Remfry.*
p. 142. SOS-SPA Kiev Press Conference. Left to right: Christian Janatsch, President of Tierhilfswerk; me; Tamara Tarnawska, President of SPA-SOS; Bohdan Nahajlo; Caroline Barker and John Ruane, Naturewatch. *Credit: Naturewatch.*
p. 143. Arriving in Ukraine with donated toys and clothes. *Credit: RdeT collection.*

Chapter 8 International Ambassador

p. 148. 1988. Dancing bear with gypsy owner waiting for tourists in Istanbul, Turkey. *Credit: Jeremy Leney.*
p. 150. 1994. Opening of the first bear enclosure at the Wildlife and Rescue Centre, University of Uladag, Turkey. This young bear arrived and was named 'Elisabeth'. *Credit: JLL/WSPA.*
p. 152. 1995. The government dog pound at Pan Chiao, Taiwan. *Credit: LCA.*
p. 152. 1995. Preparing for the WSPA Pet Respect Conference in Taiwan. Left to right: Mandy Thompson; Joy Leney; Taipei official; me; Kevin Cope. *Credit: LCA.*
p. 153. 1995.Wu Hung demonstrating a dog catching wire on me. *Credit: LCA.*
p. 153. 1995. Meeting at Taiwan Council of Agriculture to discuss the stray animal problem. Left to right: Mr. Lin Hsiang-nung. (Deputy Minister/Chairman); me; Joy Leney(WSPA). *Credit: LCA.*
p. 154. 1999. WSPA exhibition stand at Crufts Dog Show. Left to

right: Trevor Wheeler; Joy Leney; Claire Palmer; Pei-Feng Su; me. *Credit: David Paton.*

p. 156. 1994. Whilst in New York, Amelia arranged for me to visit LEMSIP: Laboratory for Experimental Medicine and Surgery in Primates, New York University Research Facility, USA. *Credit: Amelia Tarzi.*

p. 159. 1996. David Barnes and volunteers receiving the dogs from the Crete Athlada Shelter at the airport in Nevers. *Credit: GAWF/RdeT.*

p. 162. 2003. With David van Gennep (Stitching AAP) during the relocation of chimps from a Château in France to AAP Centre in Holland. *Credit: David Barnes/AAP.*

Chapter 9 The Tide is Turning

p. 166. 1962. John MacFarlane showing me the humane stun guns brought by him to France, from the USA. *Credit: Studio Rosardy, 122 Rue la Boëtie, Paris.*

p. 168. Campaigning with PMAF and HSI in France. *Credit: RdeT collection.*

p. 169. 1992. In my kitchen with Utopique a rescue horse, who regularly came in for an apple! *Credit: Jon Bradley.*

p. 178. 2002. Toto the chimpanzee lived alone in a wooden packing case which was little more than a metre wide. He was kept in chains at Chile's Circus Konig, where he had lived for twenty years. Toto was rescued by ADI and taken to a sanctuary in Africa where he joined a family of other chimpanzees. *Credit: Animal Defenders International.*

p. 179. 2003. Toto with his new family at the Chimfunshi Wildlife Orphanage, Zambia. *Credit: Animal Defenders International.*

p. 179. 1996. Elephants chained at the Monte Carlo Circus Festival – sadly a typical sight at circuses around the world. *Credit: Animals Defenders International.*

Chapter 10 Influence and Inspiration

p. 186. 2000. David Tang at a Budhist Temple in Myanmar. *Credit: David Tang.*

p. 188. 1964. With André Malraux, French Minister for Culture. *Credit: R. Delhay, 30. Avenue Aristide-Briand 30, Stains (Seine), C.C.C. Paris.*

p. 190. 2000. With John Walsh, WSPA International Projects Director, at a WSPA fundraising event in London. *Credit: WSPA.*

p. 191. 1995. With Master Wu Hung at *Refuge de Thiernay. Credit: RdeT collection.*

p. 193. 1994. With Christine Stevens, founder of the Animal Welfare Institute, Washington DC, USA. *Credit: RdeT collection.*

p. 195. 1981. Visiting Mother Teresa's Centre in Bombay, India. *Credit: RdeT collection.*

p. 196. 1981. Bombay, India. Visiting a Centre for disabled people (back row, 4th from left) *Credit: RdeT collection.*

Chapter 11 Yesterday, Today and Beyond

p. 200. 1997. The day I found Panchiao, the 'love of my life' at the Pan Chiao dog pound in Taiwan. *Credit: WSPA/LCA.*

p. 205. 2008. With Dr Jean-Pierre Kieffer, President of l'OABA at his office in Paris. *Credit: JLL.*

p. 206. Receiving the Chevalier de l'Ordre National du Mérite awarded by the President of the French Republic in 1979. *Credit: CNPA.*

p. 207. 2006. Dr. Andrew Rowan presenting the HSU/HSI Award for Extraordinary Commitment and Achievement. *Credit: HSUS.*

p. 208. 2000. Spain. Examining a galgo which was found hanging from a tree. *Credit: GINB.*

p. 208. 2001. At a conference with veterinary students in Manila. *Credit: HSUS.*

p. 209. 2006 EXPO Dallas. Having fun with friends after the conference. Left to right: Ken Grant, Sherry Grant, Neil Trent, Jack Reece, me, Victoria Kizinievic, Yuli Weston. *Credit: HSUS.*

Chapter 12 In Conclusion

p. 215. 13 December 2001. Friends arrived unexpectedly for my 80th birthday, having arranged a surprise party for me at a restaurant in Nevers. It was a wonderful day and I was amazed when Wu Hung appeared from under the table as I had no idea he was in Europe! *Credit: RdeT collection.*

p. 216. 1997. At *Refuge de Thiernay* with some of my staff: Odile Clément with Jaunet, me with Fu-lee and Nadège Darneau with Panchiao. *Credit: RdeT collection.*

p. 217. 2000. Marie-Christine Thelliez, Administrator at *Refuge de Thiernay. Credit: RdeT collection.*

p. 218. 2008. Nico Joiner, Canine Carer at Canterbury Dogs Trust Rehoming Centre. Nico came to help us at *Refuge de Thiernay* and adopted 'Cooper' a sad, thin dog who was brought into the Refuge after years of neglect. Nico and Cooper now live happily together in the UK. *Credit: RdeT collection.*

p. 219. 2009. With my great, great nephews and niece. Manuela, Tiago, and Alexis who all love animals. *Credit: RdeT collection.*

Every effort has been made to contact the copyright holders of the photographs reproduced in this book. The publishers would be grateful to hear from any copyright holders we have been unable to trace.

Acknowledgements

THANK YOU to each of the following individuals for their help and support:

- Jenny Seagrove, for her Opening Tribute
- Professor Donald M. Broom for the Foreword
- Dr Andrew Rowan for the Epilogue
- Jim Worlding, Director of Reality Images, for his expertise in restoring the photographs used in this book
- Ed Egan for providing tape recordings of interviews
- Audrey Burns Ross for her advice and support during all stages of this book
- Deepashree Balaram for editing and proof reading
- Amelia Tarzi for final proof reading
- Léopoldine Charbonneaux for translations
- Other contributors: David Barnes; Mireille Broedes; John Callaghan; Josiane Cœuret; Dr Jean-Pierre Kieffer; Cherry Mitchell; Tim Phillips; Jenny Remfry; John Ruane; Pei-Feng Su; Victor Watkins; Ghislain Zuccolo (PMAF)
- Staff and volunteers at *Refuge de Thiernay*, friends and family members for their support

Elisabeth de Croÿ:
A Tribute

Sometimes, someone enters your life and within minutes you are in love. Not in a 'let's live together and share a life' way. No, it's much bigger than that. You are in love with their soul, their vivacity and everything that they stand for. Such a person was Elisabeth. She was unique and quite wonderful and I loved her.

To spend time in her company was to be at the centre of a

Credit: Gill Shaw

To you all at Thierway. from
your biggest fan. with love —
Tommy S.

hurricane, such was her energy and her drive; but a hurricane with such a warm wind of kindness blowing through it. She'd ring me from France, demand to know if I was in a play that she could come and see when she was in town and then invite herself to tea and cakes in the garden. This was really just code for a plotting session of what she/I could do next, for the animals in dire circumstances all over the world. She was tireless. One minute she was in London; giving lectures; advising politicians or as I said, plotting. The next she was in Taiwan freeing dogs or in Ukraine changing hearts and minds.

And in between all of this she was running her own sanctuary for rescued animals, in France at *Refuge de Thiernay*, into which she had put every last penny or euro that she possessed. It was bursting at the seams, but she couldn't turn them away. Somehow she made room for them, nursed them, fed them and neutered them.

And that's how she was: larger than life and a force of nature.

I hope that in reading this book you will meet Elisabeth and fall in love with her as I did. I hope you will be inspired by her, laugh with her, and cry with her. And most of all do something, however small, for the animals she so loved.

Jenny Seagrove

Foreword

Donald M. Broom, Professor of Animal Welfare, Centre for Animal Welfare and Anthrozoology, Department of Clinical Veterinary Medicine, University of Cambridge, UK

A small number of people devote much of their energy and resources to noble causes such as attempting to improve animal welfare. Occasionally, they continue to do so for over forty years. Princess Elisabeth de Croÿ not only did this, but gave up many aspects of a privileged and comfortable life to achieve her objectives.

She describes some of her exciting encounters with famous and influential people during her early life. They range from Henri Matisse and Salvador Dalí to King Farouk of Egypt, Orson Welles and John and Jackie Kennedy. Even at that time, the glamorous young Princess Elisabeth could sometimes have valuable influence on behalf of animals. She relates how, when she met the president of Chile, her expression of horror at hearing that a bullfight was to be staged there resulted in his declaration that it would be the last in his country. There are also descriptions of many major events in world history as Princess Elisabeth wrote reports on Hungary just after the 1956 uprising, the Franco-Algerian war with its various atrocities and the war in Biafra.

The founding in 1968 of the *Refuge de Thiernay* was a significant event in the history of animal protection in France. Elisabeth explains how the concept of animal welfare was almost completely unknown in the 1970s, not just in rural France but in most parts of the world. In setting up the Refuge, some advice was obtained from the RSPCA in Britain and volunteer veterinary nurses came from Britain to help. One innovation in her efforts to minimise the worst problems of stray, often diseased, animals that were brought to the Refuge was to arrange for neutering by staff at the renowned veterinary school in the University of Lyon. At the time this practice was thought to be just a drop in the ocean of stray dogs and cats but it has proved to be of great importance in reducing the numbers of starving, diseased and wildlife-consuming dogs and cats. An interesting ethical question is raised here. Is depriving these animals the possibility to reproduce justified by the reduction in the poor welfare of their offspring and other animals? Readers can come to their own conclusions. Another innovation, later taken up nationally, was to tattoo, and later microchip each animal that passed through the Refuge. In considering such difficult issues, Elisabeth became involved with the World Society for the Protection of Animals and was invited to become one of its Advisory Directors. In her account, she pays tribute to the pioneering work of Graham Fuller who changed the concept of what an animal shelter could do in his work at Wood Green Animal Shelters during the 1980s and early 1990s.

My personal experiences of Elisabeth started when I gave lectures on the scientific assessment of animal welfare twenty years ago at meetings of WSPA or at universities in Belgium and France. She made clear her delight that there was at last a Professor of Animal Welfare and she strongly encouraged further development in this scientific discipline. I think that she was also pleased that I could lecture in my somewhat inadequate French. Elisabeth was by origin, and by penchant, very much an internationalist and after having some success in France she wanted to spread the civilising influence to other countries in Europe and elsewhere. She was encouraged by Mike Seymour Rouse to become involved with Eurogroup for Animal Welfare in its early years. This organisation, later a consortium of all major animal welfare organisations in Europe that was taken forward under the leadership of David Wilkins and Sonja van Tichelen, is now the major lobbying body on welfare matters that is listened to by the European Commission and the European Parliament.

I was well aware of Elisabeth before I met her because of the leg-hold trap issue. In 1989, Stanley Clinton Davis, a member of the European Parliament, contacted me in Cambridge to request that I should prepare a brief scientific report on whether or not such traps would have the effect of causing poor welfare in the trapped animals. The key issue that I considered in my report was the degree of poor welfare that would be considered acceptable in the legislation on animal experimentation or on humane slaughter. My report was presented in the European Parliament. At the same time Princess Elisabeth de Croÿ was an influential figure arguing the case in the corridors of the European Parliament building in Strasbourg. The result was a ban on the import of furs from animals caught in inhumane traps. This, and a similar experience relating to the killing of baby seals on which I also wrote a report, changed the views of many in the animal protection movement about animal welfare science. It was realised that a good quality scientific report by independent animal welfare scientists was of great value in efforts to change laws. In Cambridge, we followed this by founding the Cambridge University Animal Welfare Information Centre that produces scientific reports on animal welfare topics for any organisation. At the same time, the European Commission set up the Scientific Veterinary Committee (Animal Welfare Section) that also produced scientific reports.

Elisabeth started from a position of influence but her greatest impact was a result of her ability to appreciate good, new ideas and to present them where they might be heard. Few aristocrats have such a wide-ranging impact on the world. Although welfare scientists can provide information to the scientific world and to governments, the real changes come about because of the changing of public opinion and the impact of carefully-considered, factually-based campaigns. The future improvement in animal welfare in the world depends very much on people like Elisabeth.

Introduction

Elisabeth, the Princess

Told largely in her own words, *Such a Nuisance to Die* aims to give the reader a glimpse of Princess Elisabeth de Croÿ's family background; a brief insight into her early adult years as part of the international jet set; and the events which led to a dramatic change in lifestyle. Known to her family and close friends as Elisabeth, or Betty, her formal titles are Her Serene Highness Princess Elisabeth Marie Claire Léopoldine Jacqueline de Croÿ et de Solre; Princess of the Holy Roman Empire but she is addressed throughout this book as Princess Elisabeth, as in her everyday life.

Princess Elisabeth was born in 1921 at Château d'Azy in rural France, into an aristocratic family dating back to the Holy Roman Empire. With castles in Belgium, Germany, France, Holland and the Czech Republic, her family tree, traced from 1147, is amongst the most elite pedigrees in the world. The eldest of eight children, she was educated at home by several governesses, before being sent to a convent school in Paris. She abhorred the closed restrictive life in the convent and longed for her freedom.

As a child growing up at Château d'Azy she often felt detached from her family and sought comfort and solace with her pet animals. She closely watched the behaviour of wildlife that lived in the grounds of the château and together with her sisters and brother, cared for many injured wild animals such as foxes, hedgehogs and birds.

A traumatic experience on a boar hunt when she was eight, opened her mind to a world where humans and animals were subjected to suffering and abuse, mainly through indifference and ignorance. She vowed that one day when she was an adult, she would challenge such behaviour and try to make a difference in the world. However, when her parents and siblings became members of the French Resistance in World War II, Elisabeth, who longed to travel, went to Paris in search of a more adventurous life. Much to the dismay of her family, she became an air hostess, a job in those days regarded by her family as akin to prostitution! She was eventually dismissed after failing to turn up for a return flight home, from Egypt to Paris – as she was otherwise occupied with the attentions of new friends and exciting opportunities. The next thirty years were full of parties, holidays and cruising with the rich and famous. She was wined and dined by heads of state, politicians and artists from the world of fashion, painting, sculpture, ballet, film and theatre. Her exquisite beauty and engaging personality attracted many admirers; a duel was even fought to gain her affection! She was invited to millionaires' playgrounds across the world, including visits to Hollywood and was a regular guest at the Washington home of Senator John Kennedy and his wife Jackie, as well as the White House when he became the 35th President of the United States of America in 1961.

In Paris, as a member of the French animal protection society *La Brigade de Défense des Animaux,* Elisabeth organised fund-raising parties with the Duchess of Windsor, wife of the former King of Great Britain who abdicated in 1936.

Although these years were indeed an exciting part of her life, several personal experiences during this period had a lasting influence, in particular an earthquake in Persia (Iran); the Algerian War of Independence; the Hungarian Uprising; the Nigerian Civil War in Biafra and the destitute in Mother Teresa's hospitals in India.

She also witnessed suffering and abuse of animals while travelling in many countries: emaciated working horses in South America; the inhumane treatment of livestock during transportation and in the slaughterhouses of India; the exploitation of wildlife just to amuse rich hunters and collectors. All these experiences and many others continued to haunt her.

Although she had equal concern and empathy for both human and animal suffering, she knew there were organisations actively concerned with human welfare, whereas at that time, there were few people in France focusing on animal welfare. So in 1968, using a small inheritance from her aunt Princess Marie de Croÿ-Solre, a Belgian war heroine in World War I, Elisabeth set up a small sanctuary for unwanted dogs in the courtyard of a farm owned by her parents, close to Château d'Azy. Two years later, her mother, Princess Jacqueline de Croÿ-Solre, gave her a modest farmhouse with adjoining land in a nearby hamlet where Elisabeth set up an animal welfare centre for stray and unwanted animals, which became known as *Refuge de Thiernay*. In those early days at the Refuge, Elisabeth had no running water, no heating, no car, no telephone, no staff and no money; a life in sharp contrast to the glitz and glamour of former days.

In 1970 *Refuge de Thiernay* was officially opened and the following year it was legally registered in France as part of Elisabeth's charity *Défense et Protection des Animaux*. During the coming years, the charity carved a progressive path in animal welfare and was one of the first organisations in France to promote animal birth control, tattooing as a method of identification and investigation of cruelty cases. In addition the charity provided support for animals in Soviet Union countries – Poland, Hungary, Romania – through the collection of equipment and veterinary supplies.

Elisabeth's determination to promote animal welfare grew as she learned more of the extreme animal abuse that appeared to be acceptable in so many parts of the world such as animals in zoos, circuses, laboratories and animals killed for their fur. She became a member of the International Society for the Protection of Animals (ISPA) and a regular visitor to UK to learn from other animal welfare organisations, mainly Wood Green Animal Shelters (WGAS) and the Royal Society for the Prevention of Cruelty to Animals (RSPCA) – the oldest animal protection society in the world.

Elisabeth was a founder-member of several organisations including the *Conseil National de la Protection Animale* (*CNPA*), a French organisation set up to address specific welfare concerns, also Eurogroup for Animal Welfare, an international organisation set up to provide expertise and advice on animal issues to the European Parliament.

In 1981 the World Society for the Protection of Animals (WSPA) was formed from the merger of ISPA and the World Federation for the Protection of Animals (WFPA) and Elisabeth became an Advisory Director of WSPA, representing the organisation in France.

As a volunteer ambassador for both WSPA and Naturewatch, a UK-based international animal welfare organisation, she travelled internationally meeting leading politicians and other government officials, urging them to introduce or to enforce existing legislation as a means of preventing the exploitation of animals in their respective countries, such as dancing bears in Turkey; the inhumane government dog pounds in Taiwan; the 'budkas' (dog/cat skinning factories) in Ukraine; slaughterhouses in India; working horses in South America and animals in zoos and circuses.

The life of Princess Elisabeth de Croÿ is a great inspiration to many people throughout the world. Never reluctant to speak out when she felt passionate about an act of abuse or cruelty, she was sometimes seen to be a controversial figure. During the 1970s she was prosecuted and fined for verbally attacking the local chief of police who was known to kick stray dogs when seeing them wandering in the streets! Every day she was either in her office at the Refuge where she tried to respond to every donation, or in the kennels, cattery, fields, or clinic doing hands-on work alongside her staff and volunteers. When the Refuge was closed, she was lobbying through letter writing and petitions, or listening to radio and TV world news to keep abreast of international affairs and welfare issues. Elisabeth supported charities to help children, the elderly and the poor and also had a particular interest in supporting fledgling animal welfare groups in China and Taiwan.

Although marching on towards ninety years of age, her fire was still burning brightly with her vision for the future of an international humane education centre alongside *Refuge de Thiernay*, where people from developing countries could stay for practical work experience and training.

However, on 4 April 2009, Elisabeth became ill and was admitted to hospital. Her life which began in a castle was destined to end at the *Refuge de Thiernay* just six weeks later, with dogs barking, cats purring, horses neighing, pigs grunting, sheep bleating and goats blaring ... all giving thanks for the life of a very special lady.

Such a Nuisance to Die, which was completed just three days before

Elisabeth became ill, does not intend to be a precise historical document, but relies upon diaries, anecdotal evidence, photographic and media documentation, to create a picture of her life experiences. Her life before the Refuge is portrayed in brief terms, just to give the reader an idea of the contrasting lifestyle in her later years.

Elisabeth, the Activist

It was 1997 and we had been in Taiwan for two weeks, visiting government officials in Taipei and Kaohsiung on behalf of WSPA. It was now 10 p.m. and we were on our way to a hotel for our last night in Taiwan. There were five of us: Wu Hung, Yu Min and Asa from Life Conservationist Association of Taiwan (LCA), Princess Elisabeth de Croÿ and me, Joy Leney, WSPA Director for Asia.

On the way to the hotel, Wu Hung decided to try to find the dog pound which was just a few miles from the town where we were staying. He knew it was likely to be located at a municipality garbage site as WSPA and LCA had surveyed seventy-two government-holding facilities earlier that year and the majority were either located at, or close to garbage sites.

Wu Hung continued driving; from the main road we turned on to a minor road which gradually became a track. He stopped the car and we all got out. We were now in an isolated area but knew from the foul smell in the air that we were close to the site. With only the light of the moon to guide us, Wu Hung picked out his route, his grey monk's robes billowing in the night air. The rest of us stumbled along the trail behind him, the dim light rapidly fading – across a field and then on to a garbage site.

The stench was sickening as we steered a path through the rotten decaying matter and open bags of stinking rubbish, where numerous rats were exploring the contents. What an unusual convoy: Master Wu Hung, a Buddhist monk; Yu-Min and Asa, two trainee Buddhist monks; me, an animal charity worker from London, and Her Serene Highness Princess Elisabeth de Croÿ, a European princess.

Wu Hung and Asa strode ahead of the group and suddenly there was a cry from Asa. We hurried to catch up and gazed in horror

Elisabeth at home

Credit: RdeT collection

1997. Chu-nan, Taiwan. Government dog pound, cages on a garbage site where dogs were left to starve to death.

Credit: WSPA/LCA

1997. Elisabeth in a cage on a garbage site at Chu-nan removing the catching wires from dogs that had been left to starve to death.

Credit: WSPA/LCA

1997. A private dog shelter in Taiwan where we took the dogs rescued from the Chu-nan government dog pound.

Credit: WSPA/LCA

and amazement at what he had found. We gasped as we stared into a square-shaped pit, some twenty feet deep, which had metal mesh panels fixed against the sides of the pit to make a cage. At the bottom there were several bodies of dogs in various stages of decay – some half-eaten by other animals. We were now standing in total darkness except for the light from two torches; the stench was overpowering and the garbage site was so eerie; it seemed as if we had stepped on to a horror movie film set.

Suddenly, our initial gasps of horror and disbelief were met with a pathetic yelp, coming from somewhere nearby. We stumbled to where the sound came from and in the dim light saw a second pit, similar to the first one containing the dead dogs. But this pit contained ten live dogs, their eyes glinting in the moonlight as they looked up at their night visitors in silence. Paper money was strewn in the pit as a 'gift' for the dogs in preparation for their next life. In the Buddhist culture of Taiwan, reincarnation is a strong belief, so the gift of paper money also served as a 'safeguard' for the afterlife of the municipality garbage collectors who had put the dogs in the pit. It was impossible to do anything for them as it was now past midnight and very dark, and we had no equipment with us, or any way of knowing if the dogs were feral or unwanted pets. We reluctantly decided to leave the situation as it was and return a few hours later once there was some daylight, so we returned to the car and travelled to our hotel for a few hours of rest and prepared for the journey back to the UK later that day. By dawn, we were back at the site, our cases and belongings in the car in readiness for our return flight to the UK.

Once again we trekked through the rubbish and stench and found the two pits seen in the dim light a few hours earlier. What a heartbreaking sight! This was a government facility for stray and unwanted dogs – no kennels or buildings – just holes in the ground. When dogs were collected from the streets in the surrounding municipalities, they were brought here. A mechanical digger would then scoop out a deep hole in the ground, and the dogs would be thrown alive into the pit where they either starved to death, or were killed and eaten by other dogs. New pits were created as required.

In the first pit there were decomposed bodies of dead dogs, some half-eaten, others covered in flies and maggots, also bodies of dogs which appeared to have died within the last few hours. We rushed to the second pit where we had seen living dogs only a few hours earlier. Ten canine heads looked up at us, including a large old German shepherd dog, a heavily-pregnant cocker spaniel, a shar pei, and a terrified cross-bred collie pup. They all had thin, catching wires tightly embedded in their necks.

'*They must be given water,*' commanded Elisabeth. Dutifully, Wu Hung rushed off to try and find some, but in the middle of this vast site, it was impossible. So Wu Hung, ever resourceful, phoned a lady in a nearby town who owned a pet shop. She eventually arrived with two female companions, three containers filled with water, dog food and feeding bowls. All three ladies were beautifully dressed in frilly, silky Chinese attire: on reflection, an unusual sight at a garbage dump!

Now how could the water bowls be lowered into such a deep pit? Suddenly, Elisabeth stated: '*I am going into the pit,*' and proceeded to straddle the edge of the 20-foot deep pit. '*Absolutely not!*' I screamed in horror. How could I possibly return to London and admit to WSPA's chief executive that I had allowed the seventy-five-year-old princess, a WSPA Advisory Director, to climb into a pit of starving dogs where she had been torn apart and eaten before my eyes?

I grabbed Elisabeth's arm, urging her to get off the edge of the pit. '*Get away, I will be all right,*' she angrily retorted, as I pleaded with her to see reason. My repeated pleadings were futile and not for the first time I witnessed the stubborn determination of this strong-minded lady. She descended into the pit with a bowl of water uttering soothing words to the upturned heads of the dogs, while the monk, the trainee monks, and the silky ladies all looked on in horror and disbelief. I hardly dared look and indeed feared the worst.

Lowering herself slowly down the side of the pit, Princess carried the bowl of water down to the bottom. The bolder dogs rushed to the water which they gulped down in a frenzied manner. The German shepherd dog immediately vomited. We all held our breath while the dogs viewed Princess with suspicion. Was she another breed of dog that had been captured? She sat silently at the bottom of the pit.

I was willing myself to remain calm, but inside my trembling body my heart was pounding wildly. I dared not make a sound in case it triggered an adverse response from any of the dogs. Princess started to edge towards the startled dogs and slowly, one by one, she succeeded in removing the catching wires which were deeply embedded in their necks. The cross-bred collie pup was terrified, screaming loudly, and threatening to bite in a half-hearted way, but eventually it allowed the wire to be removed, while the other dogs watched with suspicion.

With water and food in the pit and the catching wires removed, I urged Princess to get out. However, her work was not yet over: '*We must get the dogs out,*' she commanded. Wu Hung and I were desperate for *her* to get out of the pit while she was still alive, but she would not budge until we agreed to try and remove the dogs as well. Fortunately, the silky ladies had dog crates in their large vehicle, so collectively we moved all of them. Apart from the occasional growl or yelp, the dogs were remarkably cooperative – and thankfully there were no injuries during the rescue, to humans or to dogs.

Time was rapidly moving on and we had to get to the airport for our flight to London, but what would happen to the dogs? Wu Hung discussed the limited options with the silky ladies. They knew of a shelter owned by a politician and quickly made arrangements for the dogs to go there. We arrived at the 'shelter' to find two long rows of cages on stilts, covered with striped plastic material. All the dogs had been de-barked – hardly ideal, but offering the best facilities available at the time. We gratefully left the dogs there, with the wonderful silky ladies promising to try and find homes for them.

As for Princess, was she courageous or crazy; compassionate or reckless?

As you read through this book, you can be the judge.

Joy Leney

1

Brief Overview of Family Background

My journey in life began on 13 December 1921 at Château d'Azy, a beautiful castle in the village of St Benin d'Azy, located in the Nièvre department of the Burgundy region in France. The village, which is about 16 kilometres from the principal town of Nevers, had a population of some 1,300 in the year of my birth and today the population stands at a similar figure.

The origins of my family claim to date back to the legend of Attila the Hun, with our family tree traced from Prince Marc of the Hungarian Arpad dynasty. Following a dispute with his brother, Marc fled to France in 1147 where he settled in the Belgian province of Hainaut and eventually married Catherine, an heiress to the barony of Croÿ. The family became increasingly powerful under the dukes of Burgundy, becoming involved in the politics of France, Spain, Austria and the Netherlands.

However, it was Jean I of Croÿ who was responsible for the family becoming supremely powerful in medieval Burgundy, when in 1397 he became the Lord of Chimay, a large area of Belgium. Although Jean was killed at the Battle of Agincourt in 1415 along with two of his sons, another son Antoine I le Grand, increased the wealth and power of the family by acquiring yet more land and titles. By the 1500s the Croÿ family had acquired land and titles throughout Europe with descendants intermarrying, so that all possessions and influence would stay within the family. In 1486 Emperor Maximilian elevated the county of Chimay to a principality and Charles of Croÿ was accepted into the Imperial Diet, the parliament of the Holy Roman Empire and just over 100 years later in 1594, the House of Croÿ was elevated to the rank of imperial princes.

1

At the beginning of the seventeenth century the House of Cröy split into four branches. However the only branch from that era and still in existence today, is Croÿ-Solre, which directly descends from Antoine I le Grand's younger brother, Jean II de Croÿ, who became the first Count of Chimay and one of the first Knights of the Order of the Golden Fleece.

Among the more illustrious family members over the years were bishops, two cardinals, several imperial field marshals, generals, governors, senators, ambassadors and thirty two Knights of the Order of the Golden Fleece.

During the French Revolution years of 1789–99, the 8th Duke of Croÿ moved the family seat to Dülmen in the Westphalia region of Germany where it remains today and the title of duke is always held by the head of the family. Among the families belonging to the Belgian nobility in the present age, the House of Croÿ ranks at the upper end of the hierarchy as it was mediatised in 1806. This means that members of a mediatised family are classed as non-ruling monarchs, with the title of Serene Highness.

The present head of the Croÿ family is the 14th Duke, Karl von Croÿ (known as Charles), with the family divided into seven main branches: three in Belgium, and one each in Germany, France, Austria and the Czech Republic.

My grandfather, Prince Alfred Emmanuel de Croÿ-Solre went against family tradition by marrying Elisabeth Mary Parnall, an English lady from an old Cornish family, in January 1875. This was considered to be a totally unsuitable match, so my grandfather was disinherited by his father, Prince Emmanuel von Croÿ, resulting in the loss of his inheritance. This included the magnificent Castle of Le Roeulx in the county of Hainaut, Belgium, one of the main residences of the Princes of Croÿ since 1429. However the marriage proved to be a true love match and brought new blood into the family, although their wealth was vastly depleted.

Prince Alfred and Elisabeth Mary settled at Château de Bellignies, in France, close to the Belgian border, and had three children: Princess Marie born in London in 1875; my father Prince Léopold born in San Remo in 1877 and Prince Reginald in London in 1878.

World War I

When Great Britain declared war on Germany on 4 August 1914, my father together with his brother Reginald and sister Marie, were living at Château de Bellignies with their 84-year-old English grandmother, who had outlived her daughter and son-in-law. Immediately my father volunteered to fight with the British Allies and Reginald would have done likewise, but Marie asked him to wait until their grandmother had got used to Léopold's absence, as she was most distressed that Britain was at war with Germany and was anxious for the future of her grandchildren. Marie, who had obtained a diploma in nursing, immediately offered Château de Bellignies to the French Red Cross as a field hospital and just two weeks later they heard that British troops would be arriving for overnight rest before marching onwards. However, fighting was soon underway and wounded soldiers began to arrive as the German occupation of Belgium took hold, with many civilians also wounded through being caught up in the conflict.

During the coming months as the war advanced, many patients arrived at the château with serious injuries that required skilful nursing. Occasionally a doctor would arrive to examine the troops, but usually Marie and Reginald, together with a small group of local people, had to make all the medical decisions. As the days went by, more and more injured Allied soldiers continued to arrive. The German army was rapidly expanding its occupation of Belgium and France and now with battles raging in the neighbouring areas, wounded German soldiers and officers started to arrive at the château in need of treatment and nursing.

The arrival of Lieutenant von Hartmann, a German officer who had been shot through the head and was bleeding profusely, caused great anxiety for Marie and Reginald. The officer had been hit by a bullet which had entered his head just above an eye and came out behind the opposite ear. Marie nursed him carefully and sat with him for days, trying to keep him still and calm, and more importantly, alive. Although unknown at the time, the Hartmann family were to repay her kindness at a later date.

In addition to the sick and wounded, many Allied refugees separated

Château de Bellignies, Belgium, the family home of Prince Léopold, Princess Marie and Prince Reginald. The tower on the left which dates from the Middle Ages, contains the hidden staircase. Photo taken after restoration following the war.

Credit: J Mercier-Hautmont (Nord)

from their battalions were in need of shelter, food and a safe passage out of the occupied territories, but anyone found assisting such people was risking at least imprisonment, or even the death penalty. So a safe place was needed to hide the Allies, but where? It was decided to use the ancient tower of the château, which dated back to the Middle Ages, as it could be accessed through an attic room which was rarely used and had very thick walls which would mask any sounds. The room was then set up as a medical store, with the door to the tower cleverly hidden behind a wall panel.

During the coming months Reginald and Marie used the tower to hide numerous Allied soldiers and often German officers were either dining or having meetings in the rooms below, totally unaware of what the tower was hiding. Marie took photographs of the fugitives which she developed so that false identification papers could be made and Reginald planned the escape routes with a small group of helpers including Edith Cavell, a British nurse in Brussels.

In December 1914, Nurse Cavell, who was the teaching director of the Berkendael Institute, Belgium's first training school for nurses,

c.1960. Prince Léopold, Princess Marie, Prince Reginald in later life.

Credit: Family collection

met a man named Herman Capiau, at her hospital in Brussels. He told her that following the battle at Mons and the retreat to Marne, many Allied soldiers had become separated from their units and were trapped behind the German front line. These soldiers, if caught, would be executed by the enemy without a trial and sympathisers would go before a firing squad. Knowing what their fate would be if caught, Reginald, Edith and Herman still continued to work out a plan for the French, British and other Allied soldiers. It was decided that the soldiers would be given refuge at the Berkendael Institute and Château de Bellignies, until they could rejoin their comrades fighting at the front. Once fit to leave, they would be given false identities and led to safety.

By mid-1915 the regular arrival and departure of men at Edith Cavell's hospital, and the visits of Reginald, began to arouse suspicion among the German authorities. They were also beginning to question the activities at Château de Bellignies. Knowing that he was now under suspicion, Reginald tried to keep a low profile, but the Germans had gathered sufficient information to show that he and Edith had played a major role in assisting Allied troops to escape from occupied territory.

Nurse Cavell was arrested on 15 August and tricked into an admission of guilt by the German interrogator, who implied that they had evidence to prove that Reginald, Marie and named others, were guilty of treason. Believing that the German authorities knew all the facts relating to the escape plans and the people involved, Edith confessed.

As soon as it became known that Edith had been arrested, word was sent to Reginald by one of their group. Knowing that he too would be arrested, Reginald immediately set off to Brussels to warn others, so when the German authorities arrived at Château de Bellignies, they were too late to arrest him. The German authorities immediately announced that Reginald was wanted for questioning and that there was a large reward for information leading to his arrest. He stayed hidden for twelve days at a friend's home in Brussels, while others made plans for his escape to Holland. He was given a false identity and a trusted guide, Henri Beyns.

For three weeks Uncle Reginald and Beyns lived in the woods

during the day, then travelled on foot by night and slept in haystacks. They hid amongst the rushes alongside the canals, then waded and swam across the river without alerting the German border guards and finally scrambled under the wire border fence into Holland.

Meanwhile Aunt Marie had been arrested, although she denied all knowledge of harbouring Allies and any escape plans. Before Reginald left they had agreed on what she should say if arrested and she kept to the story, agreeing that injured soldiers had been given medication and care at Château de Bellignies, but as the château was under the control of the Red Cross, the nationality of wounded soldiers was not of any concern to her. She was taken to the prison of Saint-Gilles to be questioned, concerning the alleged harbouring of a French pilot, of which she had no knowledge but she was still imprisoned for the crime of harbouring Allied soldiers. A few days later Marie was distraught when given the news that her grandmother had died.

Aunt Marie's trial began in October 1915 where she was found guilty of high treason and sentenced to ten years' hard labour in a German prison camp. Nurse Edith Cavell was sentenced to death and was shot just two days later. Uncle Reginald was found guilty of high treason and condemned to death 'in absentia'.

Following the trial, Marie was imprisoned at Siegburg in Germany where she became very ill. She was eventually transferred from the prison to Clemens Hospital in Munster after intervention from Pope Benedict XV, the King of Spain and the Archbishop of Cologne, Cardinal von Hartmann – the uncle of Lieutenant von Hartmann, whose life she had saved through her careful nursing at Château de Bellignies.

After her release from prison in November 1918 following the end of the war, Marie returned to Château de Bellignies to find her beautiful fifteenth-century home almost in ruins. The house was filthy and there was no glass in the window panes; the grounds which were littered with munitions and rubbish had large craters caused by the bombing; even an unexploded bomb was embedded in the floor of the dining room. But after the events of the past four years, her dilapidated home which by now had been taken over by English military, the 1st Battalion of the Bedfordshire regiment, was the least of her worries, as more importantly she was alive and free. Aunt

Marie told me in later years that the day she returned home she sat at the table in her home with a group of strangers (the English soldiers) and silently reviewed the past four years. She felt rather like *Alice in Wonderland*; bewildered.

Following World War I

Edith Cavell's dog, a Belgian sheepdog called Jack, went to live at Château de Bellignies until he died from old age, in 1923. His body was preserved and given to the Imperial War Museum in London where it is on display alongside a photo of Edith Cavell. At the end of the war, Cavell's body was exhumed from Belgium and returned to her homeland where it was re-interred at Norwich Cathedral. Several soldiers she helped escape across the frontier, stood in silence as the bishop pronounced the blessing, remembering how she sacrificed her life to save theirs.

A lamp that was used by the group to help guide more than 250 soldiers through the woods to freedom, was given to me many years ago by Aunt Marie and recently I donated the lamp to Peterborough Cathedral where there is a memorial plaque for Edith Cavell, as she was once a student teacher in French language studies at Laurel Court in the cathedral precincts.

My father, his sister Marie and his brother Reginald, who were all decorated for their heroism during the war, were remarkable people and tales of their devotion to their families and countrymen have inspired me through the years.

Following the war, Aunt Marie who was also decorated at a private investiture by King George V of Great Britain continued to live at Château de Bellignies with her dogs Foxy, Vicky and Edith Cavell's dog Jack and she remained unmarried. Reginald resumed his career as a diplomat and in August 1919 was appointed First Secretary at the Belgian Legation in Washington DC, USA. He married Princess Isabelle de Ligne in 1920 and they had two daughters, Yolande and Diane – Diane now eighty-two, still lives at Château de Bellignies. Léopold married Jacqueline de Lespinay in October 1918 just after World War II ended and they eventually had eight children, of whom I am the eldest.

8

Château d'Azy

My great-great-grandfather on my mother's side, Count Denys Benoist, was born into a family of the French nobility in 1796. His father was the Minister of the Interior and a Member of the Royal Privy Council and his mother was a painter at the Louvre in Paris. In 1822 Denys married Amélie, daughter of Brière d'Azy, and settled in the Nièvre department of the Burgundy region, where his father-in-law was a wealthy landowner and industrialist, also one of the early pioneers breeding Charolais cattle.

Denys loved the area and bought the old Château du Vieil Azy at St Benin d'Azy, with 6,000 hectares of land where he created a wonderful estate. He was primarily a businessman and started to industrialise the Nièvre where he developed the mining industry, set up steelworks and built the railway. He was the Member of Parliament for the Nièvre and Cher and had a strong social conscience, but his proposed law to introduce welfare support through social security was not supported by other politicians. He was ahead of his time.

Much of the Nièvre was wild and underdeveloped at this time, with more than 1,200 wolves and more than 5,000 wild boar roaming freely. But as Denys had made plans to develop the area, he decided that the wild animals had to be controlled. So he bred strong, swift horses for hunting and a pack of fearless hounds: hunting wolves and wild boar became a serious activity. It is said that Denys killed the last wolf in the Nièvre in the early nineteenth century when hunting on his favourite horse.

Denys decided to build a new château and toured his land with two men and a ladder to find the best position and view for the castle, and then he hired the best architect he could find, Monsieur Delarue. There were many artisans living in the area so Château d'Azy which was started in 1846 and took five years to build, was built entirely by local people. The castle was built over four floors with towers at each of the four corners. Over the doors carved in stone were sculptures to symbolise the activities of the family: a railway; a beehive to represent industry; a hammer and pick for the mining industry and heads of Charolais cattle.

On the ground floor was a huge hall with an enormous chandelier and a grand sweeping staircase, built in the style of the Renaissance period. At each of the four corners of the hall were doors leading to circular rooms; one of these rooms at the front of the house was the Winterhalter room where many of his paintings were displayed. Above the doors in the drawing room were paintings by Van Loo representing the arts: music, architecture, sculpture and painting and above the doors in the dining room were paintings by Boucher, representing the four seasons, with six paintings of hunting scenes from the London Exhibition of 1849 adorning the walls. Portraits of family ancestors were hung in the dining room, where eleven of the portraits were painted by Rubens. In 1884, a beautiful chapel was added to the original building and was built into a circular room at the front of the house, opposite the Winterhalter room.

Denys' eldest son, my great-grandfather Count Paul Benoist d'Azy, followed in his father's footsteps and continued to develop the work of the mines, the steelworks and the railways in the Nièvre and he was also active in both local and national politics.

The village of St Benin d'Azy had been practically destroyed during the French Revolution, with looting and regional uprising commonplace, so there was plenty of rebuilding and renovation work for him to oversee.

Like his father, Paul too had a strong social conscience and was known to show as much concern for his workers as for his business interests. In 1856 Paul married Claire Jaubert, the daughter of Count Hippolyte François Jaubert, a French politician and botanist and they lived at Château d'Azy. They used their home as a centre for social activities; as an arts centre for painters, musicians and as a centre for debating ideas for social reforms. Paul and Claire's daughter, Marie-Thérèse Benoist married Zénobe, the Marquis de Lespinay and their daughter Jacqueline (my mother), was born in March 1889.

In 1918 Jacqueline married Prince Léopold de Croÿ-Solre and my mother's parents gave them Château d'Azy as a wedding present, which became our family home in the Nièvre. It is still in the family and is now the home of my nephew Henri and his family.

Family Life at Château d'Azy

My parents were well matched: my father Léopold was good looking and confident and my mother Jacqueline was beautiful and graceful, but more importantly they were very much in love and remained so throughout their forty-seven years of married life. My parents settled in their new home and eagerly awaited the birth of children and three years later, their first child, me, arrived into a loving home. I was named Elisabeth Marie Claire Léopoldine Jacqueline, fondly called Betty by the housemaids and other staff.

In January 1933, my father succeeded in legally reclaiming the legal rights which were taken away from his father, Prince Alfred Emmanuel, when he married Elizabeth Mary Parnall. Although Alfred had been disinherited by his father Prince Emmanuel von Croÿ in 1875, it was not deemed to be a legal act, so all privileges that accompanied the titles were restored, but alas few of the family assets, as by then they had been passed down to other relatives.

My nurse and nanny during my early years was Nurse Henderson, a British nurse who was appointed through a London agency. She was a formidable, yet kindly soul who was capable and firm and I am told that she quickly established a warm and close relationship with me and life moved on smoothly. The arrival of a second child, Princess Marie Dorothée Constance Marie (Mimi), was quickly followed by the arrival of Claire, Léopold, Florence, Catherine, Jacqueline-Rose (Rose) and Emmanuela (Mella) with finally, a ninth child, stillborn. All of us were born within an eleven-year period.

My parents employed more than ninety staff to ensure the smooth running of the home, the care and tuition of the children, the grounds, woods, chauffeurs, general maintenance and gardens. Grooms attended to the horses and hounds with a team of huntsmen for the actual hunts and the head chef was responsible for the cooks, scullery lads and kitchen boys.

All the children loved nature and animals and we cared for any injured animals we found in the grounds of the château; birds, hedgehogs, rabbits, foxes. I could not bear to see ladies with fox fur around their shoulders as was the fashion in those days; the glass eyes of the dead animal seemed to come alive staring at me appealing for sympathy.

1934. Prince Léopold de Croÿ-Solre, my father.

Credit: Family collection

c.1925. Princess Jacqueline, my mother.

Credit: Family collection

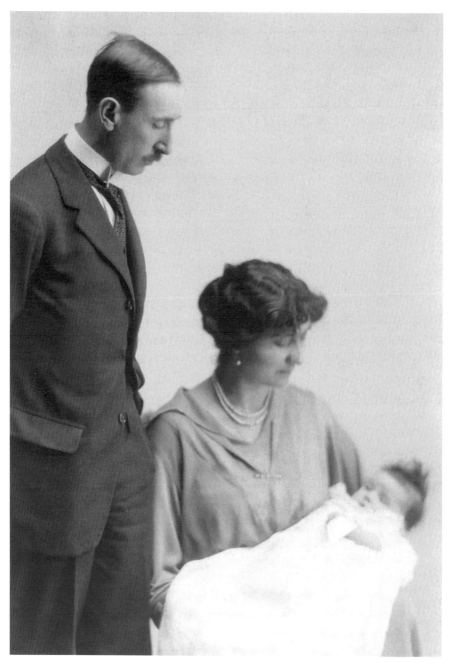

1922. Me, aged 1 month with my parents Princess Jacqueline and Prince Léopold.

Credit: Family collection

1925. Nurse Henderson, my wonderful nurse.

Credit: Family collection

As time passed, my sisters and I were schooled by a succession of British governesses, but we were all headstrong with somewhat rebellious personalities, so were not always easy to manage. Although we became bored with formal learning, such as reading, writing and mathematics, we all acquired a passion for art, literature, classical music, opera and ballet. We were taught many European languages and all learned to converse fluently in English, German, Italian, Flemish, Dutch, Spanish and of course French. My brother however had a different education to his sisters, more structured and wide ranging, as at the time it was considered more important to educate sons than daughters.

The château with its large dark rooms provided many exciting hiding places for us, but our favourite was out in the open on the rooftop which we could reach from the third floor windows. Sometimes our nannies would be searching for us and they would freeze in fear and disbelief as they spied us sitting silently on the rooftop with our legs dangling over the side. They were even more alarmed when we crawled along the gutters from one room to another. On more than one occasion, when feeling upset with one of my sisters, I even threatened to jump off the roof.

My father often worked overseas in his role as a diplomat and I loved the times when he came home. He would gather us around the piano and we would all sing English songs with such gusto, such as: 'What shall we do with the drunken sailor?' and 'Little brown jug'. But eventually our carefree days at home ended when the time came for each of us to go to a convent boarding school, Sacré Cœur, near Paris. I hated it!

The strict regime of convent life proved a stark contrast to our privileged existence at Château d'Azy. We were not accustomed to socialising with anyone other than those from a similar background and we were used to having servants to wait on us, so at the convent we were in a very different environment, one that was dominated by religious indoctrination and harsh rules. I longed for the holiday periods when I could return to my home and go with my family on holiday to Belgium.

I enjoyed the holidays we spent with our cousins, the daughters of Uncle Reginald. I remember a holiday with them in Morocco where Reginald was a minister (now known as an ambassador) at the

c.1932. On holiday with my sisters, brother and nanny (5th from left).

Credit: Family collection

Belgian Embassy. My cousin Diane was about six at the time and she had a favourite small religious statue. To tease her, my sister Mimi and I, who were several years older, hid the statue and told her that the devil had taken it. Later we heard the poor child praying aloud: '*Dear Mr Devil, would you please return my statue…*' What horrid children we were to tease our small cousin and how strange that one can recall such simple happenings from so many years ago.

During our teens and early twenties, my sisters and I were included in some of the occasional parties that my parents hosted at the château, a welcome addition to the daily routine of exercising the horses, walking the dogs and reading. However when World War II was declared in 1939, life changed for us all. I was now almost eighteen

Immediately my parents offered Château d'Azy to the Red Cross as my mother had trained as a nurse during World War I, also my parents and some of my sisters, especially Mimi and Claire, became active with the French Resistance and both drove ambulances and delivered messages for Allied soldiers. However I found the whole concept of the war confusing and I did not want to take sides, after all, many of our relatives were German.

17

1932. My sister Marie Dorothée and me (right) with our maternal grandmother, the Marquise de Lespinay.

Credit: Family collection

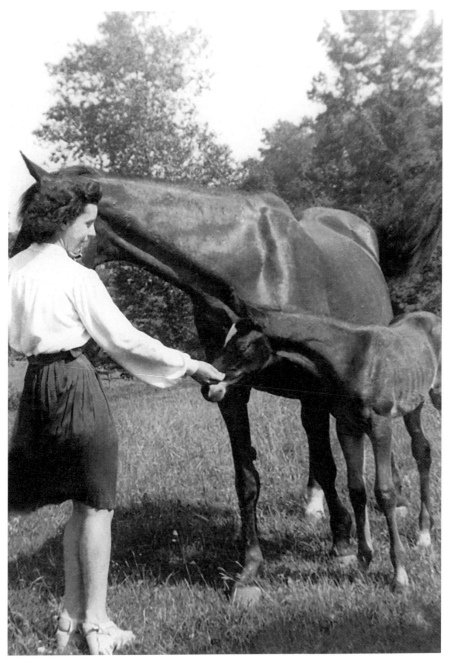

c.1937. Me with Miniska and her foal.

Credit: Novaphot. 4. Rue du 14 Juillet, Nevers

c.1945. My sisters, left to right: Princesses Claire, Marie Dorothée, Catherine, Florence, Jacqueline-Rose, Emmanuela.

Credit: Studio de France, 3. Rue du Colisée, Paris. Ely 17–96

The château became a place where Jewish children were hidden from the Gestapo. In France and Belgium, as part of Germany's ethnic cleansing policy, Jewish families were taken from their homes and put into concentration camps. Often children were hurriedly sent to stay with friends before their parents were arrested and were kept hidden until the Resistance found safe houses where the children could live. I recall twenty-five Jewish children living at the château. How traumatic for these poor children to be separated from their parents, especially as many of them would never see their families again. To my knowledge, only a few of these children were eventually reunited with their parents after the war.

As the war moved on, English soldiers were parachuted into the countryside surrounding the château and the children would shout, 'God Save the King', whenever a jeep turned up. However when the United States forces arrived towards the end of the war, the children, not knowing the difference between the English soldiers and the Americans, also sang and shouted 'God Save the King', annoying some of the Americans who thought they were indeed quite different to the English.

Meanwhile my Uncle Reginald, who had been condemned to death in World War I, had become a Belgian diplomat in Sweden. As Sweden was a neutral country, he was safe there, but Aunt Marie who still lived at Château de Bellignies was once again suspected of hiding Allied soldiers (she had been imprisoned for such activities during World War I) and was arrested along with her chauffeur, Yvon, who was badly beaten by German interrogators in an attempt to force a confession. My aunt, who by now was in her mid-sixties, was allowed to return home after being questioned. Yvon was also released. As Aunt Marie was so frail and crippled with arthritis, the interrogators probably thought she was incapable of any activities with the Allies … little did they know.

At the end of World War II

On 4 September 1944 towards the end of the German occupation of France when the German soldiers were retreating, one of the villagers in St Benin d'Azy threw a hand grenade which wounded two German soldiers. Panic broke out and the soldiers started to round up all the local people, including the Mayor and his staff, and locked them in the village toilets. The terrified hostages could do nothing other than peer through the small windows which were shaped like a heart, a club, a diamond and a spade.

A young apprentice boy working in the bakery saw what was happening and ran through the fields to Château d'Azy to inform my parents. My mother immediately put on her Red Cross uniform and with my father left the château to see what help they could give. However there were German soldiers at the gate and they arrested my father, but they did let my mother go to help the wounded soldiers.

When she arrived at the scene my mother quickly assessed the state of the wounded and speaking in German, agreed with the officer-in-charge that a doctor was needed urgently. There was no doctor available close by and no car either, so the officer instructed a soldier to take my mother on his motorcycle to find our family friend Dr Franck Bernard.

As she had never been on a motorcycle before, my mother leaned the wrong way when cornering, almost causing an accident and making it a hazardous journey for the driver and herself. It was indeed a great surprise for the villagers to see my mother riding pillion on a German motorcycle, as they thought she was the most dignified woman in the world! Dr Bernard was also surprised to see my mother on a motorcycle clutching the German soldier's back, but realised this was an emergency situation and immediately came to attend to the wounded soldiers. He then took the soldiers to Nevers General Hospital in his car.

As no one owned up to throwing the hand grenade, the incarcerated hostages were lined up to be shot. My mother stood alongside them and protested strongly. She said that these honest village people would never be so foolish as to throw a hand grenade at German soldiers. My mother would not move out of the line of fire and the officer-in-charge, eventually worn down by my mother's protests, ordered the hostages to lead the German soldiers through the woods to their base-camp at Château Chinon 40 kilometres away. He said they would serve as protection for his soldiers on the journey and deter any possible further attacks by local people; if his men arrived at their base-camp unharmed he would release the hostages.

The relieved villagers were eventually released and returned to St Benin d'Azy footsore and weary, but before returning to their homes, they came to Château d'Azy where my father had now been released and each personally thanked my mother for saving his life.

About seven years later, my mother was awarded the French Legion of Honour for her courage. This award was created in 1802 by Napoléon Bonaparte and is the highest award given for outstanding services to France. The presentation was made by François Mitterand, who was Minister of Justice at that time.

Life after World War II

All my siblings developed interests which gave them rewarding lives and careers. Mimi became a world-renowned expert on farming issues, especially Charolais cattle which she judged in many countries, including America, Thailand and Brazil. She was also an accomplished musician and in later life opened her home to many aspiring artists and gave concerts at her home Mânoir de Valotte. Julian Lennon, the son of legendary Beatle John Lennon, stayed at Mimi's home in 1984 and wrote his first album there, giving it the title 'Valotte'.

Claire assisted Mimi in her early years in agriculture and later farmed in Scotland with her husband. She became a sculptor and exhibited in galleries all over Europe and made models of some of my pet dogs which are proudly displayed at my home.

Léopold attended university in Louvain and later became a corporate barrister. For his services in World War II he was decorated with the *Croix de Guerre*.

Florence became an accomplished pianist, attending the University of Music and Performing Arts in Vienna. She was a keen advocate on care of the environment and belonged to a club in Brussels where leading experts were invited to present their opinions and scientific findings.

Catherine, who lived at the château all her life, worked for the

Ministry of Foreign Affairs as an interpreter and public relations officer for guests of the French government at home and overseas.

Rose trained as a nurse and cared for abandoned children at the Abbé Pierre centre in the suburbs of Paris. Following her marriage, she moved to Portugal where she ran an antiques business with a friend. She also established Hostesses of Portugal, the first tourist organisation in the country providing interpreters, guided tours, and professional childminders for tourists.

Emmanuela became a painter, with many of her creations displayed in overseas galleries. She was an accomplished horsewoman and won international trophies for her equestrian skills.

2

Spreading My Wings

Living at Château d'Azy became rather dull and uninteresting for me as I longed for travel and adventure. So during World War II I left home and worked in Paris for one year as a trainee nurse, but found this life to be almost as restrictive as my schooldays in the convent. There were many rules to observe and I hated being shut in at nights, so on occasions I would jump out of the window and look for adventure with new friends, but it was wartime and people were understandably cautious.

Following the end of World War II in 1945, my opportunity to travel came when I decided to become an air hostess. My family was horrified as they regarded such work in those days as little more than high-class prostitution and it was a major embarrassment for them. Once when I was working on a flight to Italy and scheduled to take the rest period at a hotel in Rome, I decided that I would prefer to stay with my Uncle Reginald who was the Belgian ambassador to Italy at the time and lived in the Vatican precincts. I telephoned him from the airport and asked if I could stay with him. He was delighted to hear from me and said he would fetch me immediately. When he saw me in my air hostess uniform he stared in astonishment and his first words were: '*Take off that ridiculous little hat.*' We travelled to his home in silence and clearly I was an embarrassment for him at dinner that evening, as a bishop and other dignitaries were dining with us; fortunately the subject of my employment was diplomatically avoided by all.

However being an air hostess did give me the opportunity to travel to countries such as Egypt, Israel, Italy, Greece and Arabia, using the few rest days before the return flight, to gain a glimpse of different cultures and to open my eyes and mind to the mysteries of the wider world.

I worked for Trans World Airlines (TWA) for about eighteen months, but my career came to an end in Cairo where I was staying for a three-day rest period, when I met a friend from the Belgian international tennis team, which was on tour in Egypt. Their schedule sounded such fun; besides playing tennis they had planned to visit the prime tourist spots and had been invited to dine with celebrities and royalty. When it was time for me to get on the plane for the return journey to France, some of the tennis team urged me to stay with them. I didn't need much persuading and decided that it would be more fun to stay with my friends, travelling around Egypt, so I didn't return to the plane and was subsequently fired by the airline.

During my travels in Egypt, I went to numerous parties and nightclubs and on one occasion was at a party hosted by King Farouk who came to the Egyptian throne in 1936 at the age of sixteen. He was about thirty when I met him and was already overweight, although my father had met him about ten years earlier when apparently Farouk was a handsome young man. Tales of the king's obsession for fine cuisine accompanied by his extreme gluttony were already a major topic of gossip, as his youthful shape and appearance had changed rapidly after he became king. He was also criticised for his extravagant lifestyle as he regularly travelled in Europe buying whatever caught his eye – even during World War II he continued to live lavishly. Although he was courteous to me I was a little wary of him as he seemed to be self-obsessed and dismissive of those around him and I had been warned of his reputation for grabbing hold of women against their wishes. I was invited to go to a club with him and his entourage after the dinner, but decided politely to decline the offer.

At a dinner party held at the Jockey Club in Cairo to celebrate the New Year, there were about fourteen of us, all laughing and throwing small paper balls at each other. I was teasing Prince Abbas Halim calling out in fun: '*I'm going to catch you!*' '*Oh no you won't,*' he responded, but just then I threw several balls at him and one went straight into his mouth and lodged in his throat. He started to cough, then to choke. We all laughed at first but then realised he really was choking. Friends rushed to his aid and at last he stopped

26

the choking noises and spat out the balls. I remember we were both rather embarrassed...

While in Egypt, I visited many historic sites. The beautiful Luxor Temple situated on the bank of the River Nile is an image which stays with me to this day, more than sixty years later. I remember gazing at this amazing grand complex of statues, columns and buildings dating back to 1400 BC, then closing my eyes and trying to imagine life in those days. I have always been fascinated by history and lifestyles in ancient times and actually standing amongst those structures at Luxor gave me a tingling feeling of excitement and the urge to see more of what the world had to offer.

But not everything was so beautiful in Egypt: one evening in Cairo when I was leaving a wedding party where guests had been eating and drinking all evening continuing into the early hours of the next day, I saw many people living in extreme poverty staring at us partygoers in awe and I felt so guilty. On another occasion in Upper Egypt I was horrified to see beggars performing the dangerous feat of jumping from a great height into the Aswan Dam. I was so moved to see such desperation and poverty and felt that I must find a way to help the underprivileged – just how to help, I was not sure, but I could hear my father saying to me these words, which he said so often to all his children when we were growing up: *always remember you were born to a privileged life ... so many are not so fortunate ... but should be helped whenever possible.*

For a short period during the early 1950s, I worked as a receptionist at the Paris office set up to develop the Marshall Plan. This was the strategy proposed by the State Department of the United States of America for rebuilding Europe after World War II, and was named after the US Secretary of State, George Marshall.

The office was in the grand building, called Hôtel Talleyrand, where my great-grandmother Countess Claire Benoist lived during the nineteenth century. As a child, she and her parents had their portraits painted by Franz Winterhalter, the German-born artist who was known as the 'Painter of the Princes' as he was commissioned to paint royalty in Spain, Belgium, Russia, Mexico, Germany, France and the UK. Her piano teacher was Frédéric Chopin, the famous composer and pianist and the chairs used by Chopin in her music

Chair from the music room used by Chopin at the home of my great-grandmother – now used by animals at my home!

Credit: RdeTcollection

c.1950. As President of the Debutante Ball getting ready for the Ball at Versailles.
Credit: Charles of the Ritz, 51 Av Montalgne, Paris – VIII

room are now in my home at *Refuge de Thiernay*, where they make comfortable seats for my aged cats and dogs.

While working there, I recall an occasion when I was asked to be a witness at the wedding of two of my work colleagues. The bride was white and of Russian extraction and her husband was a black American. The couple were very much in love with each other, but a mixed race marriage was rare in those days in France and the couple faced strong opposition from family and friends, so I was one of just four guests at the wedding. Thankfully, sixty years later, attitudes opposing mixed race marriages have changed and now such a union is not at all unusual in France.

In 1953 I was offered the most exhilarating job of my life when a close friend, Denys Scott, hired me to organise the publicity for 'Salut à la France', an extravaganza of music and art to be held in Paris. Denys was Director in France for J. Walter Thompson, an American advertising company with an office in a very chic part of Paris, Rue de la Paix. Although it was operating successfully in the

1950. Preparing for the Debutantes Ball at the Palace of Versailles.

Credit: Louis Peltier, actualities Eclair Continental, 38 rue Victor-Basch 33, Montrouge

USA and London, it had failed to make an impression in France so 'Salut à la France' was an ideal opportunity for J. Walter Thompson to shine and indeed for me.

It was such an exciting international event with artists taking part from all over the world including Louis Armstrong, the world-renowned jazz singer, George Balanchine's New York City Ballet with his wife the ballerina Tanaquil Le Clercq, and the Philadelphia Orchestra under the brilliant leadership of Eugene Ormandy. I went to the ballet every night and made so many lasting friendships with people from the USA. My favourite performance was Gershwin's 'Porgy and Bess', which I watched at least ten times, the haunting music overwhelming me on each occasion.

I enjoyed working in promotional work and public relations, as it seemed to come easily to me. During the 1950s, I was President of the Débutante Ball, an annual event held at the Palace of Versailles providing an opportunity for selected young ladies to present themselves in their finery at this society event. Eligible young men were also invited to the Ball, so it was hoped by each mother that Cupid would match her daughter with a suitable beau, preferably rich. It was never discussed in such a basic way of course, but in my opinion it seemed to be one of the main reasons for holding the event.

I was responsible for the organisation, invitations and administration, including arrangements for the guest of honour to officially open the Ball. I remember that one year, Alix de Foresta, Princess Napoleon from the Imperial House of Bonaparte, was the guest of honour. Everything went so smoothly and she officiated with such grace and style, as befitted the occasion.

From the mid-1940s to mid-1970s, I was able to travel extensively at the invitation and generosity of many high-profile people, including royalty, heads of state, actors and artists, staying at some of the most luxurious homes and hotels in the world. In those days I was considered to be an attractive young lady with an 'hourglass' figure, so was asked to model clothes created by the leading fashion houses in France at the numerous parties, receptions and banquets I was attending. I had a wonderful time when I went to the USA for two weeks as an ambassador of goodwill for the Spanish designer Miquel Ferraras. If I wasn't socialising or at a party several times a week, I thought something was going wrong in my life.

c.1960s. Wearing a cat mask at an Embassy party in Paris.

Credit: Y. M. Pech, 322 Rue Saint Jacques, 322 Paris-V

c.1950. On a skiing holiday at St Anton, Austria.

Credit: Foto Rio St. Anton am Ariberg

c.1952. With friends on the beach in the Bahamas.

Credit: Vega Keane

Christian Dior, my favourite designer, was considered to be the most influential fashion designer of the late 1940s and 1950s. He dominated the fashion scene after World War II with his 'New Look' range featuring the voluptuous hourglass silhouette. People in the public eye such as the actress Marlene Dietrich, Princess Margaret and the Duchess of Windsor, all loved to wear Dior fashions, so the Dior label accounted for a significant amount of France's haute couture exports.

One of my favourite Dior creations was a full length pale pink silk dress with golden ears of corn shimmering from the delicate material which I wore to the fashionable Travellers' Club Ball on the Champs-Elysées in Paris. Suddenly I saw another lady wearing an identical dress which was more unfortunate for her as she had probably paid a substantial price for the dress, whereas mine was on loan!

Pierre Balmain, who opened his fashion house in 1945, was another of my favourite French designers and I was one of his early models, promoting his new styles at the parties I attended. Balmain was a brilliant costume designer and created costumes for many legendary

34

films and revues including creations for Katherine Hepburn in *The Millionairess*, Josephine Baker's 1964 *Revue*, and films starring Brigitte Bardot, Vivien Leigh and Mae West.

From my early teenage years I was a great lover of the arts and was fortunate to meet such eclectic people from the world of ballet, theatre, music, painting and sculpture. Salvador Dalí, the eccentric Spanish artist, lived in Paris and my sister Catherine knew him well as he painted a portrait of her. He was brilliant in an arrogant, outrageous way, but I found him to be a strange, unnerving person although indisputably gifted. In addition to being a painter he was also a sculptor, and even used his genius in the field of fashion design working with the Italian fashion designer Elsa Schiaparelli, grandmother of Marisa Berenson, the American model and actress.

Dalí also designed jewellery and created a fabulous range with a brooch called the Royal Heart which was purchased by an American millionaire, Cummins Catherwood, for his wife Kathy. It was so elaborate. It was gold, encrusted with forty-six rubies, forty-two diamonds and four emeralds, and gave the illusion of a heart beating. I remember holding a cocktail party for 300 people at my tiny apartment in Paris and Kathy Catherwood came, wearing the Royal Heart. Her jewels created a great talking point, as several society magazines at that time were featuring her jewellery on their front covers. Many people were so envious of Kathy that evening and I was of course delighted that Dalí's famous design was 'on show' at my cocktail party.

I met Dalí several times at dinner parties and on one occasion went to his hotel room with a friend. To my horror he had a pathetic-looking leopard cat lying on the sofa – it was wearing a beautiful diamond studded collar and had painted claws. I felt so sorry for the poor creature as from my childhood days I have always felt strongly opposed to any wild animal living in a domestic environment. I looked at it carefully and suspected that it was drugged as it could hardly move and just stared at me with glazed, unseeing eyes.

I also recall meeting the artist Henri Matisse while driving with the Cuban ambassador from Paris to the south of France. I was on my way to stay with Countess Simone Sanjust di Teulada, the daughter of Mme Jean Stern, the successful racehorse owner. Her horses were

c.1950. Party girl!

Credit: RdeT collection

c.1953. Wearing a fur coat before I knew better!

Credit: Eddy van der veen, Rue Choron, Paris

magnificent and two of them won the coveted *Grand Prix de Paris*: Sicambre in 1951 and Phaeton in 1967.

I met Simone through my volunteer work with the French animal welfare organisation *La Brigade de Défense des Animaux*. We became good friends after visiting Monaco to meet Prince Rainier on behalf of the Paris Guide Dogs for the Blind. Simone was always great fun and had so many stories to tell. She was Jewish and during the war her husband, Count Sanjust di Teulada, kept her confined to their home in Italy, well hidden from the Germans. She also had a fabulous house at Roquebrune-Cap-Martin with a private beach, about 2 kilometres from Monte Carlo where she had a small basic animal shelter and held parties at her house to raise funds for the shelter. Her friend, Estée Lauder, founder of the famous cosmetics company was often there and donated cosmetics for fund-raising.

On the way to Simone's home, we stopped at Henri Matisse's studio to look at some of his work. He was probably the most well-known artist of the twentieth century, and we discussed his wonderful project, designing and painting the glass windows at Chapelle du Rosaire in Vence near Cannes. He started this work in 1947 and it took about four years to complete. I remember him as a charming man with a quizzical expression and pointed beard, and we stayed in his company for about three hours before continuing on our way. Later I was upset to discover that I had lost my new Polaroid camera on the journey – very modern technology in those days.

I met many people from the film world and was introduced to Jean Renoir at a dinner party at a publisher's house in Paris. He was the son of the famous impressionist painter Pierre-Auguste Renoir and was the subject of many of his father's paintings. Jean was an acclaimed actor, author and film director, making films from the silent era to the end of the 1960s. He lived in Hollywood before the war, but returned to France to support his country, so he was well respected in France.

I also recall meeting a good friend of his when I was working as an air hostess, the actor, author and film director Orson Welles; we were on the same flight and part of my job was to be attentive to the passengers. He was rather a heavy man, not attractive in appearance, but with an amusing personality and we discussed so many topics,

c.1960s. Reception at the Belgian Embassy, Paris. Ex-Queen Marie-Jose of Italy (left) speaking with me and an Embassy official.

Credit: R. Delhay, 30 Avenue Aristide-Briand 30, Stains (Seine) Paris

ranging from politics to pigs ... literally. His most famous film was probably *Citizen Kane*, which he directed and acted in and is still to this day considered by certain film critics to be the best film ever made.

I have always admired the naked human form, male and female, when shown in a tasteful artistic context and in my home today there are several nude drawings of me made by my friend, the artist Dan Rasmusson. I posed for Rasmusson in St Tropez, also in my apartment in Paris and many of his drawings were sold in the USA after being exhibited in Philadelphia and New York. However, in my opinion, Rasmusson's best work was created specifically for me in my apartment in Paris where he painted dramatic murals of wild horses on the walls of my lounge, giving the small room an elegant romantic aura.

Over time I became more and more enchanted with ballet and at a reception held at the Indian Embassy in 1953, I was introduced to the world authority on ballet, Bengt Hager from Sweden with his

1962. Reception at the Belgian Embassy, Paris.
Queen Elisabeth of Belgium (left) me (centre).

Credit: Photographiques International, Agence L.A.P.I. Les Actualities,
R. Delhay Director Bureau, 9, Cour Petites Ecuries, Paris-X

c.1960s. Reception at the Belgian Embassy in Paris. L to R: Baroness Yolaine de Candé, Baroness Jaspar and me.

Credit: R. Delhay, 30 Avenue Aristide-Briand 30, Stains (Seine) Paris

Indian wife, the ballerina Lilavati Devi. When we were formally introduced, Lila smiled at me and said: '*But I've known you all my life.*' Of course we hadn't met before but immediately there was a bond between us and that was the beginning of a lifelong friendship – sadly Lila died in 2002. Fortunately, I have wonderful memories of some of the unique experiences we shared, especially the Festival of Dance tour of India in 1976 which I outline in a later chapter.

During the 1950s I developed what was to become a lifelong interest in politics, not just for French politics but also the international scene. Through the years I went to many political meetings and rallies in France and the USA, eager to learn more of world affairs. At one stage in my life I seriously considered a career in politics, but always seemed to be enticed away from France through opportunities to travel. But when Charles de Gaulle became President of France in 1958 with plans for a new constitution, Jacques Baumel, Secretary General of the Gaullist Party suggested to me that I should form a

41

1964. Executive Committee of the First World Festival of African Art, left to right: President Léopold Senghor of Senegal, Duchess of Rochefoucauld, me (President of the Committee), André Malraux, Minister of Culture.

Credit: Photo by J. Campbell

Ladies Political Club to try and stimulate more support for new reforms and I eagerly accepted the challenge.

Unfortunately it was not easy to persuade women to join a political group in that era, regarding it as a 'male interest', so I decided that to get the club off the ground, I needed to open it to men also. This I did and the membership quickly grew in numbers to more than 200 men and women. I realised later that a mixed-sex political club was a progressive initiative at that time, as historically women were seldom represented in political circles.

My family was already well known in political circles as my father and other relatives had held key roles during World Wars I and II and various official government positions following the war periods. For example, my father was a royal envoy before World War II which covered duties such as being sent to countries to inform other governments of a royal event; his brother Prince Reginald was an

42

ambassador by career. As detailed in an earlier chapter both brothers and their sister Marie were active in helping the British Allies during World War I and my parents were active members of the French Resistance during World War II.

Throughout the 1950s and 1960s, I was a regular guest at the Belgian Embassy in Paris and became great friends with the Belgian ambassador and his wife, Baron and Baroness Marcel Henri Jaspar, especially as we shared a love of animals. During World War II, they lived in London and once found a bedraggled kitten sheltering from an air-raid during a storm. They cared for him, kept him as their pet and called him Blitz, eventually taking him with them when they moved to their next ambassadorial posting.

I was honoured to be at a reception held in 1962 for Queen Elisabeth of Belgium, wife of King Albert I as Queen Elisabeth was a friend of my Aunt Marie and was a great support to Marie when she was released from prison at the end of the war.

On the day of the reception I first had to meet Mr John MacFarlane from the USA who was bringing some humane stun guns into France for use in abattoirs. I met him as arranged and then had to hurry to the Belgian Embassy. The security staff on duty were certainly confused and just a little anxious when I arrived for the reception carrying guns!

I also attended a reception at the Belgian Embassy in honour of the former Queen of Italy, Queen Marie José (Queen Elisabeth of Belgium's daughter) who was the last Queen of Italy, as the monarchy was abolished in 1946. My sister, Princess Catherine, was chaperone for her daughter Princess Marie-Gabrielle and my sister Rose, was *dame de compagnie* to her youngest daughter Princess Marie-Béatrice.

When the President of Chile visited Paris in 1965, I was invited by the French Ambassador, Christian Auboyneau, to join them for lunch at the Embassy. In conversation I mentioned to President Eduardo Frei Montalva that I was concerned to learn from friends in Santiago only that morning that a bullfight was going to be staged in Chile. At the time Chile was the only country in South America free from this horrible spectacle. He listened to my concerns and seemed unaware of any such event in his country, but said that he totally disapproved of bullfighting and if it was happening in Chile, he would make sure that this would be the first and the last in Chile. The scheduled bullfight was stopped and to my knowledge up to the present day, there have been none in Chile.

As a guest at the German Embassy in honour of the visit from the Chancellor of West Germany, I was standing in a doorway thinking how small in stature Chancellor Adenauer looked next to President de Gaulle, when he, Adenauer, turned to pass through it. Just as I was about to move, he clutched me around the waist and lifted me to one side without saying a word. I was so surprised at his lack of formality.

The First World Festival of African Art was planned to take place in Dakar in 1966 and a planning committee was formed in Paris in 1964. The executive committee, of which I was the president, included President Senghor of Senegal; Duchess de la Rochefoucauld and André Malraux, the French Minister of Culture.

Léopold Senghor became the first President of Senegal when the former French colony of Senegal, on the west coast of Africa and part of the Mali Federation with French Sudan, claimed independence on 20 August 1960. Senghor was educated in France, but he remained true to his roots and was a freedom fighter for Africa. During World War II he fought with the French Resistance and for a short while was a German prisoner of war.

During the 1930s, Senghor, together with Aimé Césaire from Martinique and Léon-Gontran Damas from French Guyana, created the concept of 'négritude', an ideology that holds black culture to be valid in its own right and not connected to colonisation in any way. It originated as a concept to promote cultural pride and emphasise the beauty of all things associated with being black and of African origin – an affirmation of African cultural heritage. Senghor was a remarkable man, a poet, a statesman and a visionary. When he died in December 2001, Senegal declared 15 days of national mourning.

The First World Festival of African Art was highly publicised and attracted black artists, performers and musicians, many with global reputations, from all continents all eager to be present at this celebration. The festival was officially opened by André Malraux with an address on African art, followed by President Senghor's address on the emotion and rhythm of African music.

Although I was greatly committed to this event, I was unable to go to Dakar to finalise preparations and to attend the festival, as my father Prince Léopold became very ill and died in December 1965, just a few weeks before I was due to leave for Dakar. My father was a major influence in my life and as the eldest child I decided I must spend the next few months close to my mother and his devoted sister, my Aunt Marie. My father's death and the following months were very bleak for me.

Life was one long party during the 1950s and 1960s with the month of August known as the month for parties in the south of France. Occasionally, they were boring (I actually fell asleep at the dinner table on one occasion) but usually I met the most fascinating people from all walks of life, such as the enchanting Her Majesty the Queen Sirikit of Thailand; Arletty, the popular, beautiful, witty French actress and Merle Oberon, the even more beautiful mixed-race film actress. I was fascinated by Merle; during the day she was on the arm of an elderly English 'Sir' and at night in the company of a prince of Yugoslavia! Prince Sadruddin Aga Khan became a great friend as we shared a mutual passion for deep-sea diving and ecological issues.

Charlie Chaplin was seated next to me at a dinner party at La Reine Blanche, the home of Paul-Louis Weiller, an extremely wealthy businessman, who seemed to know everyone. Chaplin was a charming although surprisingly shy dinner partner and our conversation was limited, but I still felt in awe of this talented, unassuming man as not only was he the most famous mime artist in the world, but also a talented actor, composer, musician and film director.

I was often invited to parties at the Monaco home of Prince Rainier and Princess Grace, but I found conversation with Princess Grace, the beautiful former Hollywood film actress, somewhat strained as she appeared to have no interest in animals. Perhaps she found conversation with me difficult as I may have spoken too much about them.

Prince Rainier had a monkey that was becoming increasingly grumpy. I felt sure it was unhappy because of its inadequate environment – permanently chained to a large rock – so I diplomatically asked the Prince if he would allow an expert to visit and advise on the situation.

He agreed, so I arranged for the expert to come from the UK and he made numerous recommendations to improve the monkey's quality of life, in particular by changing its living quarters. Sure enough, once improvements were made, the monkey became less unhappy and easier to handle.

In contrast to many casual acquaintances from my party days who were indifferent to animals, I remember Ingrid Bergman, the Swedish actress as a great animal lover. She was so famous for her role in the 1942 classic *Casablanca* but very modest. I met her several times, the first was in 1964 at the Swedish Embassy when I invited her to the Christmas party charity event I was helping to organise for *La Brigade de Défense des Animaux*. She came and showed interest in every single animal, especially a scruffy little dog with the saddest eyes, who had been sexually and physically abused. The poor little thing had marks from cigarette burns all over his body. She was horrified to hear his sad story, but very happy when I said he was about to be adopted by some people I knew who lived close to my home in the country and that I was taking him to his new home the following day.

There was an unexpected twist to this story as within an hour of arriving at his new home, the dog escaped and later that day turned up at the door of Château d'Azy where I had briefly stopped before taking him to his new home. It seemed he wanted to be my dog and as he had been clever enough to find his way to my home, how could I possibly part with him? I couldn't and he stayed with me for the rest of his life. I named him Gri-Gri which means 'lucky charm'.

Another animal lover, the French actress and singer Edith Piaf told me that she couldn't sleep when she heard of animals being mistreated. Piaf was one of the most popular French entertainers of her era, but she had a difficult private life with much personal sadness, so found solace in her love for animals. She was minute in size, only about 4ft 8in. (143 cm) with large, sorrowful eyes, but somehow she radiated strength of character. I took a friend to one of her shows. He had been captured and tortured during World War II and had lost his eyesight. After the show I took him backstage to meet Piaf who had also been blind as a child from the age of three until she was seven, following the onset of keratitis. Fortunately, the condition eventually improved and she regained her sight. She was able to empathise with my friend's situation and was surprised to learn that his guide dog 'Marquis' was a Dalmatian, an unusual breed for such a role.

I often stayed in Cannes, in the south of France and on one occasion met two brothers at a party who were friends of an American friend of mine. They were extremely wealthy American businessmen and were about to hire a yacht to cruise from Cannes to Capri and would I be interested in joining them? '*Why not!*' I responded.

We set sail accompanied by Rex Harrison, the English actor probably best known for his role as Professor Higgins in the film *My Fair Lady*. I didn't warm to him as he seemed rather short tempered, but his wife, the actress Kay Kendall, was very sweet.

Kay and I had lots of fun; we swam together, sunbathed, played cards and strolled around the magical Isle of Capri.

Within a few days, one of the brothers asked me to marry him but I was not even tempted – although he was so rich. At that time in my life my aim was not to find a husband, but to travel and visit all corners of the world, so I certainly had no time to become a dutiful wife.

A few years later while holidaying with a friend in Corsica in the Mediterranean, we realised we were anchored alongside Jacques Cousteau, the French scientist and explorer. My companion immediately recognised Cousteau as he and his ship *Calypso* were both already well known.

Jacques invited us aboard *Calypso* and asked if we would share some wine with him which he had retrieved from a Greek ship, found lying on the seabed. The wine was in an urn which he estimated to be 2,000 years old. I would try anything in those days, so welcomed a taste of this ancient wine, but did it make us ill? Well no, it didn't, actually it was rather tasteless and we all survived. I was not sure if Jacques was playing a joke on us, or whether the wine had really come from an ancient urn on the seabed, but somehow, I think it was true.

Cousteau later became the most famous marine author, scientist, ecologist, film-maker, and underwater researcher in the world, working on many of his studies from *Calypso* which was fully equipped as a mobile research laboratory. With Emile Gagnan, a French engineer, Cousteau was the co-inventor of the aqua lung, a diving suit that enabled safe underwater exploration. Having met him, I followed his illustrious career over the years through the media, with avid interest.

A most exciting place to be invited to stay was the millionaires' playground, Eden Roc, a luxury hotel in Cap d'Antibes in the south of France. I stayed at the grand home of Fritz Mandel, the Austrian industrialist but was also invited to use the facilities at Eden Roc, as well as the luxury pools and homes of neighbours. All the neighbouring properties were owned by multi-millionaires and famous names – one well-known owner was Jack Warner, president of Warner Brother Studios in Hollywood. At the time I thought it was absolutely wonderful to bask in the splendour and opulence of their lifestyle. What a contrast to my lifestyle today!

I also met Joe Kennedy when partying at Eden Roc. Father of the now legendary Kennedy family, he had been the US Ambassador to the UK from 1938–1940 and was a leading member of the US Democratic Party. While chatting with him I told him that I had been to the USA and was longing to go again. Much to my surprise, a few weeks later an air ticket arrived from him as a present for me. I used the ticket but did not meet him again until a few years later when we met at the home of his son, the US Senator John Kennedy, later to become President Kennedy.

3

The Lure of America

Christmas Parties for Animals

On 20 January 1936, King George V died and his son Prince Edward became King Edward VIII of Great Britain. Edward's girlfriend at the time, whom he wanted to marry, was the American socialite Wallis Simpson and she was in the process of divorcing her second husband.

The monarch is the Supreme Governor of the Church of England and at the time, the Church of England did not allow divorced people to remarry, so Edward could not remain as the king, if he married Mrs Simpson. By wanting to marry a twice-divorced American, he created a constitutional crisis.

During an emotional broadcast to the British nation on 10 December 1936, King Edward VIII stated ... *'I have found it impossible to carry the heavy burden of responsibility and to discharge my duties as I would wish to do, without the help and support of the woman I love...'*

He abdicated and his brother George succeeded him, becoming King George VI, father of the present monarch, Queen Elizabeth II.

Edward was given the title of Duke of Windsor by his brother and married Wallis Simpson on 3 June 1937 at the Château de Candé in France. They lived in France during the pre-war years and again after World War II and became part of high society life during the 1950s and 1960s. They were seen by some people as celebrities, as they regularly hosted parties and travelled between New York and their beautiful Paris home in the Bois de Boulogne.

The Duchess of Windsor was a great dog lover, owning several pugs and during the 1960s she was a patron of the *Noël Des Bêtes Abandonnées*, the Christmas parties I helped to organise in Paris, to raise funds for *La Brigade de Défense des Animaux* and to find homes for unwanted dogs. The Duchess was not beautiful, not very tall, but striking and elegant, lively, with great presence and charm and always beautifully dressed. Even in a crowded room she stood out and enjoyed the limelight. The Duke however was a very different personality. When I visited their home he would stay discreetly on the balcony listening with apparent interest, but remaining silent; also on occasions such as receptions at the embassies, he seemed to prefer to be in the background. When we did have a conversation, we talked about horses and dogs.

The first *Noël Des Bêtes Abandonnées* in 1964, sponsored by Mars, the company that produced Canigou dog food and Ronron cat food, was held in two large marquees and it poured with rain. I remember the Duchess who was officially opening the party, arriving in high-heeled black galoshes, wearing a sleeveless black Dior dress with a white ermine fur coat … oh dear, in those days we did not understand the suffering of animals hunted or farmed for their fur. The event was widely reported in the press and the dog food company was delighted when one picture showed the Duchess, Father Christmas and a tin of its food, clearly displaying the brand name. I must confess that this was quite by chance, although I was given the credit as I was responsible for arranging the media coverage and it was a wonderful scoop for the dog food company.

People who supported the event included Madame Georges Pompidou, wife of the French Prime Minister; government officials, ambassadors, politicians, actors and veterinarians. Elisabeth Arden, founder of the cosmetics company, donated some magnificent Christmas decorations for the parties, which I still have at home and use each year to decorate the office of the Refuge.

At the Christmas party the following year, the Duchess of Windsor adopted a griffon-type stray dog which she named Pompidou, after the Prime Minister. The following day, a leading newspaper ran a story with the amusing headline:

'*When the Duchess of Windsor takes Pompidou in her arms*'

United States of America

I longed to visit America and as a young person was fascinated by it and all things American, especially the glamour and glitz of people in the fashion industry, politics, film and theatre. I got to know an American called Jacqueline Bouvier through a mutual friend, when Jackie was a student in Paris from 1949–50. Jackie, the daughter of a wealthy Wall Street stockbroker, was from New York and we quickly discovered that we had several common interests, especially art and fashion. Jackie loved France, spoke fluent French and studied for a year at the University of Grenoble and the Sorbonne in Paris. We met at parties and I remember an amusing occasion when we went to the races together and shared binoculars. I had to keep adjusting

1964. Duchess of Windsor with TV Presenter Léon Zitrone (left) at the Christmas Party for Animals in Paris.

Credit: Paris-Jour. Michel Hermans

51

1965. At the home of the Duchess of Windsor, Paris to organise the Christmas Party for Animals.

Credit: Paris-Jour/Michel Hermans

them after Jackie used them as her eyes were so wide apart! We shared a love for Dior clothes and Jackie always looked so elegant and stylish. When she left Paris she invited me to visit her in the USA but as so often happens when one is young with many friends and places to go, we did not stay in touch.

In 1953 I got my first opportunity to visit the USA through a travel agent friend. As a 'thank-you' for recommending his Paris agency to friends and other contacts, he gave me an air ticket to the USA – I was so excited! Stephen Millett, an American lawyer I knew in Paris arranged for me to stay with his friends Joy and Foxy Carter in Georgetown, Washington DC and I was on my way. I had planned to stay in the USA for a few weeks but ended up staying three months.

I also stayed with Molly Tackleberry McAdoo in New York. She was in the fashion industry and her husband was involved in politics. Another friend took me to many places where I could buy exquisite dresses for just one or two dollars: I was in heaven. A memorable highlight was visiting film studios in Hollywood and trying on Elizabeth Taylor's dresses!

1972. Christmas Party for Animals. Left to right: Dr Méry (Founder of CNPA), SPA official; me, Mme Messmer (wife of the Prime Minister).

Credit: : Photo Patrice Picot. Jours de France

It's strange how certain abstract memories stay in one's mind, as I recall clearly how one afternoon I went to a Broadway theatre on my own to see the musical, *Carmen Jones* and found myself sitting next to a black lady. At the end of the show she turned towards me and asked if I had enjoyed the performance. '*It was simply perfect and Carmen was brilliant,*' I replied. She gave me a radiant smile and said: '*Carmen was played by my daughter.*' I was invited to go backstage to meet her daughter and the cast and eagerly accepted. It was a wonderful afternoon.

I went to so many dinner parties and social functions in America during visits over the next ten years and met many famous Hollywood stars including Gregory Peck, Sydney Poitier, Jane Fonda, Henry Fonda, Roger Vadim and Jean Seberg, to name just a few. On one visit to New York a huge electronic sign had been erected in Times Square, boldly displaying this message: 'New York Welcomes Princess de Croÿ!' Another memorable occasion was the 1962 ball, 'April in Paris', which was held in New York at the Hotel Pierre. It was the place to be seen. It was glamour at its best: the dresses, the decor, the music, the food, the atmosphere, were simply perfect.

It was on my second visit to America in 1956 while staying with Joy and Foxy Carter that I met Jacqueline Bouvier again. Jackie was now Jackie Kennedy, wife of Senator John Fitzgerald Kennedy (Jack) and she invited me to their home, Hickory Hill, Virginia. This was a beautiful property located in the countryside outside Washington DC which had previously been the Union Army headquarters of General George B McClellan during the Civil War. I went to Hickory Hill for dinner two or three times a week and met so many fascinating people at their home, actors, artists, media personalities, academics and politicians, including Jack's brothers Robert (Bobby) and Edward (Teddy). When the Kennedy family were together, the atmosphere was electrifying, each person seeming to be more amusing than the other when telling hilarious tales. Some, I suspect, were spontaneously invented for the occasion.

The Kennedy family was very warm and kind to me. We exchanged many opinions and shared concerns for social issues such as race and poverty, debating for hours and hours; they were very happy days for me. I was loaned an old jalopy, also a house opposite the University

1962. At la Belle et la Bête charity dog show.

Credit: Apis-Paris 43 Rue de Trevise. Photo Daniel Conde

of Georgetown and it was arranged for me to sit in on history lectures to learn more about America. One morning I was waiting for a lecture to begin and was sat next to a black man. Suddenly, a white man rushed up to me and asked me if I would like to move: '*No thank you,*' I replied, '*everything is just fine.*' Such was life in the USA at the time, with an apartheid system not dissimilar to South Africa's, but fortunately such attitudes are rapidly changing and now, more than fifty years later, both countries have black presidents.

On another visit, Teddy, Jack's youngest brother, was asked by Jack to accompany me to the Harvard Museum of Natural History in Cambridge, Massachusetts, as I was so keen to see the collection of *Glass Flowers* made by Leopold and Rudolf Blaschka in Germany. Teddy appeared to be very bored and clearly not interested in the

1961. We win 1st prize at la Belle et la Bête charity dog show.

Credit: R. Dehesdin. Studios Vendome-Flash, 12 Place Vendome, Paris

museum, or perhaps he had been several times before. Still, he had to spend the whole afternoon listening to me enthuse about the incredible art collection. He was patient and courteous, but I suspect he would have preferred to be elsewhere! I did not get to know him as well as the other brothers, as he was much younger and had younger friends and interests.

On 20 January 1961, Jack became the 35th President of the USA and in his inaugural speech he made this famous statement to encourage patriotism: '...*Ask not what your country can do for you; ask what you can do for your country.*' He quickly became a popular president, raising the hopes and expectations of the underprivileged. Jack, Jackie and I remained friends during the coming years, meeting at parties and social gatherings, and I was also their guest at the White House. I found Jack to be a compassionate man and a champion of the underdog, also with an eye for a beautiful woman.

On one of his visits to Paris, Jack was a guest of the French President, Charles de Gaulle. Parties were traditionally held for heads of state at the Elysée Palace in Paris, the official residence of the President of France. At the official reception for the Kennedys, to which I was invited, Jack suddenly saw me and called my name out loudly across a crowded room. President de Gaulle appeared so surprised; he was far too grand for such casual behaviour. However I was amused to see de Gaulle's reaction, as I was now used to the relaxed style of American behaviour compared to the rather stiff, European protocol and knew that de Gaulle would be rather shocked.

I also got to know two close friends and colleagues of Jack, George Smathers, a lawyer and politician who represented Florida for eighteen years and Torbert (Torby) MacDonald, a politician from Massachusetts. George was so handsome and charming and lived up to his nickname of Gorgeous George. He was one of Jack's close confidants, travelling with him internationally as well as in America. Torby MacDonald was also a charmer and great fun. Jack and Torby were lifelong friends having been room-mates as students at Harvard and Torby was also an usher at Jack and Jackie's wedding in 1953. Finally, he had a very sad duty to perform, as a pallbearer at Jack's funeral.

On 22 November 1963, President Kennedy was assassinated, at the age of forty-six while on a political visit to Dallas, Texas. Shock

1961. Showing the 1st prize trophy to Marquis.

Credit: RdeT collection

1962. Leaving Paris for New York to attend the 'April in Paris' Charity Ball
at the Hotel Pierre.

Credit: Pan American World Airways Overseas Division. NY. International Airport

and disbelief reverberated around the world. It is often said that everyone remembers where they were and what they were doing when they heard the news of President Kennedy's assassination and I remember clearly where I was when I heard the terrible news.

I was driving to the south of France for a political meeting with Prince Jean de Broglie, former French Secretary of State for Public Service. The radio was on and we were half listening as we chatted. Suddenly the dreadful news hit us – President Kennedy had been shot. I was absolutely stunned; I could not believe what I was hearing. My thoughts darted from Jack to Jackie and their two young children, then back to Jack, his parents, his brothers and sisters, then again to Jackie and the children.

Over the next few days I listened avidly to further news reports, to the theories and details of what had happened and of course the burning question: why had it happened? I recall listening in disbelief day after day as I could not bring myself to accept the tragic news. I relived the fun and happy times I shared with the Kennedy family and I felt full of sadness for them all, as their lives had now changed forever.

Another tragedy hit the Kennedy family five years later on 5 June 1968 when Bobby Kennedy was assassinated in California. Also a brilliant politician, Jack's younger brother championed the cause of the anti-apartheid movement in South Africa and in 1966 as senator for New York, he visited South Africa with his wife Ethel and his aides. At the University of Cape Town he delivered the Annual Day of Affirmation speech on 6 June 1966 and made a stirring address: '... *Each time a man stands up for an ideal or acts to improve the lot of others, or strikes out against injustice, he sends forth a tiny ripple of hope.*'

Such a remarkable address was so motivating for the South African students as it sent out a strong message in support of racial equality. The quote is engraved on his gravestone in Arlington National Cemetery, Washington DC where he is buried next to his brother Jack.

Bobby, who was eight years younger than Jack, always seemed in earnest with a strong commitment to racial equality. I have since wondered if he really was a 'boy scout' or did he have links with

1962. A sign in Times Square, New York, USA to welcome me!

Credit: RdeT collection

the Mafia as widely rumoured? I have no reason to believe such rumours and although I never related to him as well I did to Jack, he was always welcoming and friendly to me.

It was such a tragedy for the lives of two outstanding brothers to have ended so abruptly. I know that many books and articles have been written and films produced relating to the lives of the Kennedy family – some controversial – but I can only comment with certainty on my own experiences with them. They welcomed me into their home with such generous hospitality, so I have only warm memories of the happy times we shared together, including the often noisy, yet always stimulating, political debates.

Sadly, during the coming years two other friends of mine were also murdered, in totally unrelated incidents. Barbara Baekeland was killed in November 1972. I met her when she was staying in France and we instantly struck up a friendship. She was a striking woman in appearance with thick, auburn hair; she was an extrovert, very warm, amusing, and thoughtful – an unusual person in numerous ways. She was an American married to Brookes Baekeland, heir to the Bakelite plastics fortune and they had one child, a son Tony.

61

1962. President John F. Kennedy, 35th President of the United States of America at
The White House, Washington DC, USA.

Credit: RdeT collection

Barbara was very fond of animals and was on the committee of the *Noël Des Bêtes Abandonnées* with me and we organised the fund-raising Christmas parties in Paris.

I spent a wonderful holiday in New York at Barbara's plush apartment in the Upper East Side and Barbara welcomed my invitation to visit the French countryside and *Refuge de Thiernay* with Tony. I remember Tony as a sensitive child with a talent for writing poetry. When he was about thirteen, he saw a crow in a cage at a pet shop in Paris. He felt sorry for the incarcerated bird so he bought it and carried it on his lap for the three-hour journey to Mânoir de Valotte, the home and farm of my sister Mimi, close to the *Refuge de Thiernay*. He then lovingly released the bird in a field on the farm. At the time this seemed to me to be a very sweet and caring gesture, but I learned later that he was not always so kind to animals.

Tony developed schizophrenia and became increasingly disturbed. When he was twenty-six he stabbed his mother to death at their Chelsea home in London. Then when he was eventually allowed to return to America, he stabbed and tried to strangle his grandmother and was sent to the high security prison on Rikers Island, New York City. In March 1981, he was found dead in his prison cell.

A book and Hollywood film, *Savage Grace* describes the true life story of the Baekeland family and how Tony as a child often behaved cruelly towards animals and insects. Such behaviour is often an early indication of a deep-seated aggressive personality trait which emerges as violence towards humans in adult life. Over the years I have learned of a variety of research on the relationship between abuse of animals and abuse of people, and I try to create awareness of this research through my *Refuge de Thiernay* magazine.

Another unrelated stroke of fate happened in 1976, while I was driving in my car listening to the radio. It was Christmas Eve and I was on my way from Paris to my family home, Château d'Azy, for Christmas celebrations. This time the news reported that Prince Jean de Broglie had been shot (he was my travelling companion on the day we heard the news report of President Kennedy's murder). Once again I felt numb with shock and disbelief and could not believe that yet another friend had been murdered. I had to pull up on the roadside to gather my thoughts and calm my racing heart before continuing on my journey. Prince Jean de Broglie was a leading figure in the French government and had been heavily involved in negotiations at the end of the Algerian War of Independence. He was also a dear friend.

Travel in South America

Having been to so many states in the USA and at the time loving all things American, I was keen to visit South America as I knew that the various countries were diverse in tradition, landscape and culture and it would be a new type of adventure. My opportunity came in 1965 when I was invited by a multi-millionaire to his home in Argentina, where he lived for part of each year. On the way I stopped off in Lima in Peru, went to the obligatory cocktail parties at the Belgian Embassy and met many people who invited me to stay any time I wanted, then after four days I travelled on to Buenos Aires in Argentina.

Once settled in Argentina, I visited the French Embassy as my childhood friend, Marguerite de Jumilhac, was married to Count Jean de Guébriant, the renowned explorer, then a diplomat at the embassy. I stayed with them for a month.

I travelled around with my friends and went to several estancias or cattle ranches and I had a narrow escape one day at the ranch of Prince de la Tour d'Auvergne. While watching the method of getting cattle into the dipping trough, I got too close and suddenly the machinery caught the seat of my trousers and for a few seconds I was suspended in the air, hovering over the trough. I was so embarrassed at the thought of falling in, but could do nothing to avoid it happening. Fortunately, the machine pulled me back and saved my blushes!

At many of the estancias I visited, I was not at all happy with the way in which the horses were handled, which was unnecessarily rough, with repeated beatings when they didn't do exactly as required. Sadly, my protests at the treatment given to the horses fell on deaf ears. Also in other South American countries I saw draught horses and riding horses in the most appalling, emaciated conditions, hardly able to stand, with their skeletal bones seeming to protrude almost through their thin, scabby skin. Yet, they were still being worked.

1965. Lima, Peru. Helping at the zoo clinic with Carmen Benavides.
Credit: RdeT collection

From Argentina I travelled to Chile where I stayed for three weeks in Santiago at the home of the French Ambassador, Christian Auboyneau. Whenever and wherever I travelled, I always tried to visit animal welfare societies and in Chile I met Godofredo Stutzin, a lawyer and founder of an animal protection group, *Union de Amigos de los Animales*, who took me to the local dog pound. It was awful! All the animals looked so wretched, thin and huddled together in small dingy pens, the cages tied together with pieces of wire and string. One small dog looked even more miserable than the others and I just could not leave him there, so I pretended that he was my dog, that he had escaped and I desperately wanted him back. We took him back to Godofredo's home where he lived until he eventually died of old age. Godofredo and I became very good friends, and kept up a correspondence over the years.

The English wife of the Belgian ambassador in Santiago was an animal lover and said she wanted to adopt a stray dog, so Godofredo arranged for us to visit a field where there were more than 300 dogs roaming around. There didn't appear to be anyone in charge so I climbed over the wire to choose one. The dogs charged at me eager for some attention and I was quickly plastered in mud from their enthusiastic welcome. I picked up a dog, holding it high above my

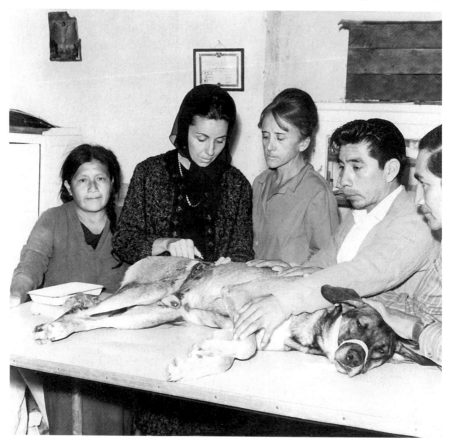

1965. Lima, Peru. With Carmen Benavides at the clinic, cleaning a dog's wounds.

Credit: RdeT collection

66

head and showed it to my friend. It was a long-bodied, grey-coated vaguely dachshund-type male and she called to me that she would take it. Fantastic, I thought, another one saved! He settled with her and became great friends with the ducks that lived on the pond in the embassy grounds.

I desperately wanted to see the lost city of the Incas, Machu Picchu, so decided to return to Peru. On arriving in Lima I booked into an inexpensive hotel, unpacked my suitcase and then phoned my friends, Carlos and Tere Gutiérrez to say that I was back. They were horrified to hear where I was staying, as apparently it was a notorious part of Lima. I was told to repack my case immediately as they were sending a car to collect me.

I stayed at their home and was taken to museums, one of my favourite pastimes, also to the wonderful ancient archaeological sites of Machu Picchu, now a UNESCO World Heritage Site. I also wanted to go into the jungle to see how the native people lived. My perfect

1965. Lima, Peru. An emaciated horse, sadly not an unusual sight.

Credit: H.R. Ramus, Fotographia commercial, Nicloas de Pierola 1014, Lima Peru

hosts were so surprised and found it hard to understand why I wanted to do this, but because they wanted me to be happy, they arranged for us all to be taken to the jungle villages. I was enchanted with the bright colours of the villagers' clothes which contrasted with the tranquil beauty of the landscape. The local people were most welcoming and we met several tribes and went into their homes which had been built from sticks, leaves and other vegetation. At a local bar, I was amused to see a very dignified local man with his pet pig on a lead.

While in Lima, I contacted Carmen Benavides, who ran a basic clinic, free for the animals of local people. Carmen, whose grandfather Oscar Benavides was the former President of Peru, was also responsible for building the zoo in Lima. I loved the simplicity of the clinic and decided to stay and help for a month. I was able to show the volunteer helpers various techniques for handling and treating the animals such as how to bandage wounds and how to give tablets to difficult dogs. Often, we met the French priest as he cared for the sick and bereaved people in the shanty towns.

I went regularly with Carmen to these towns to treat animals where onlookers would cry out in alarm: '*Don't touch the dogs, they may have rabies.*' Today, more than forty-five years later, rabies still exists in some South American countries, although rapid strides have been made to eradicate it in recent years. Rabies also exists in many other parts of the world, yet it is a preventable disease so need not exist. Fortunately, in 2005 the Alliance for Rabies Control was set up to prevent it occurring in humans and animals, with programmes for implementation worldwide, *with the vision of a world where all countries have eliminated rabies.* So in the near future, it should be confined to the history books.

I was taken to see a zoo near Iquitos; it was appalling and possibly the worst zoo I have ever seen, with animals appearing to live in perpetual distress as they paced up and down, round and round, in an agitated fashion. We also went to a roadside café where the owner had a private collection of animals; again the conditions in which the animals lived were totally inadequate. I can recall in particular an alligator living in a box which was secured to the river bank, the box being barely longer and wider than the reptile itself. Other miserable animals were dotted around with about twenty visitors excitedly laughing and pointing at them. I could not contain my thoughts and spoke loudly to the visitors: '*Do you really think this is so funny?*' There was a surprised silence, only broken when a lady spoke up and said: '*No it isn't funny, it's horrible.*' Another person then spoke up in agreement and together we discussed how traumatic life must be for each of these unfortunate animals.

On leaving the café, I saw a lady with a squawking chicken that was being carried upside down, its feet bound together to make an improvised carrying handle. I smiled at her and showed her by demonstrating with an imaginary chicken how the animal could be carried securely by tucking it under one arm. She cooperated and walked on with the chicken under her arm nodding her head as a sign of understanding. Was she just humouring me and would she revert to her usual practice of carrying the chicken upside down? Perhaps she would, but I have found on many occasions that speaking up for animals can make people stop and think and perhaps just now and again, it has the desired effect as the following story illustrates.

One day when my sister Rose was working at the children's home in Paris, the Abbé Pierre Centre, a small boy there was idly pulling the wings off a fly and a grasshopper. My sister Rose saw this and chastised him severely, explaining that he was behaving cruelly towards a harmless creature. Many years later, he came to visit us at Château d'Azy and said that Rose had made such an impression on his young life that he had never forgotten her lesson. He was now a film director in America, making films on nature and the environment.

When the time came to leave Peru, I moved on to La Paz, the Bolivian capital. Travelling by train, I met a young man who was on his way to a retreat run by Christian priests. He was most surprised to find a young lady travelling on her own, as this was very unusual in South America in the mid-1960s and he insisted on escorting me to the French embassy. The French Ambassador in Bolivia, Monsieur Ponchardier, was the brother of the admiral I worked with in Algeria in 1956, during the Algerian War of Independence. Although he was very busy and could not take time away from his duties to escort me, he arranged for me to meet the President of Bolivia the following day. However a few hours before the meeting was scheduled to take place, the president was deposed.

The ambassador gave me the use of a car and driver so with some new friends, two Peace Corps escorts and a freelance photographer, we decided to go immediately to Brazil to visit the new capital city, Brasilia. The former capital, Rio de Janeiro was located along the south east coast of Brazil, but the new city of Brasilia, (with modern architecture in contrast to the old Portuguese style of architecture) had been created closer to the centre of the country and became the new capital in 1960. I loved the vibrancy of Brazil, although I encountered a strange, unnerving experience at a night club in Rio, where women were put into a trance. I felt strangely excited and how I wished I could have stayed longer at that club.

On the day I was due to return to Paris, I was with friends on the Copacabana beach in Rio, when one of the group realised that the car keys had disappeared. Time was moving on fast and we had to get to the airport. In desperation, Don Juan Orleans-Braganza, a member of the imperial family of Brazil held the plane back for us and waited until we eventually found the keys, after an extensive search of the beach. There are times when it is useful to know the right people!

As a going-away present from South America, one of my friends gave me two Inca skulls more than 1,000 years old, found on an archaeological site in Peru. I keep them displayed on a chest of drawers in my guest bedroom at *Refuge de Thiernay*, where they always provoke conversation and on occasions, alarm, from nervous guests.

Although I loved the mysteries of the ancient world found in the South American countries, I was troubled by the poverty and hardship of the daily lives of so many people living in the shanty towns, also by the apparent acceptance of abusive treatment to animals. My mother was a staunch Catholic, believing fervently in the teachings of the Catholic Church and in South America I found people with similar strong beliefs, but personally I struggled to accept a God who allowed such widespread suffering.

I loved the magic of Peru in particular and could have stayed longer with my friends, but for family reasons I returned to France.

4

Life Changing Events

The Wild Boar Hunt c.1929

As children, my brother, sisters and I were taught never to make a fuss, never to complain and always to keep our feelings to ourselves. So I shared my feelings with my dogs and horses, also the foxes that we tamed and over time developed great affinity with all animals.

I can recall being horrified at the way in which animals were treated in rural France during my childhood years in the 1920s. I felt so sorry for the hunting dogs, incarcerated most of the time, huddled together in small pens. If they were injured, their wounds were just pulled together with large safety pins. The pigs were killed so cruelly, tied on to slanting boards and their throats slit using sharp knives, screaming in agony until their death throes subsided. I can still hear the screaming in my mind.

The cattle were routinely beaten when loaded on to vehicles, regardless of whether they were cooperating or not. The poor chickens were crammed into small wire cages and sent hundreds of miles on trains to other parts of France, the journeys often taking several days and no food or water given on the journey. Of course, many were dead on arrival. Why were these lovely animals treated so badly, I silently questioned.

The first life-changing event that I can recall is still a vivid memory for me although it was almost eighty years ago. I was about eight and that day was important to me, as I was the guest of honour at the boar hunt. I was riding my horse Babette in the company of about twenty huntsmen, all smartly dressed in their fine green hunting jackets, with smart matching riding breeches. Even at such a young

71

c.1929. St. Benin d'Azy, getting ready for the boar hunt.

Credit: Family collection

age, I knew that whatever happened that day I had to be brave and ride my horse fearlessly, and keep up with the adult riders, otherwise my parents would be disappointed in me.

We gathered at the meeting point; the hunting horn signalled the start of the hunt and we were off. The horses with their riders galloped across the fields with sixty strong hounds howling and barking excitedly. After a short while the hounds picked up the scent of a wild boar and the huntsmen responded to the sound of the horn which signalled we should ride in pursuit of the prey. The boar was frantically trying to outrun the hounds and I was willing him to escape, but eventually the hounds tracked him down and caught up with him in a frenzied mass, circling the poor animal until it was surrounded with no way of escape.

The hounds moved in for the kill as the panic-stricken boar, near to collapse through exhaustion and fear, fought bravely, but one boar against sixty hounds was such an unfair match and the defence-less animal was soon lying motionless on the ground. I was trembling in despair while overwhelmed with sadness for the fate of the wild boar.

It was dragged away by the hunt workers and later that day one of its paws was presented to the guest of honour. As I was that guest, I received the paw of the wretched animal, dripping with blood! I was stunned, my mind and body numbed by the murderous act and the subsequent presentation of the paw, all in the name of tradition. I was heartbroken; I could not speak. In my childlike way, I vowed to myself that one day I would protect wild boar and all other animals and I would teach people to treat animals with kindness and love.

As a child I felt unable to criticise adults as my upbringing taught me to respect them and never to complain or criticise, but in my heart I knew that the behaviour of the huntsmen that day was totally wrong. I remember making a silent prayer for the boar and asking God to make him well again and happy in heaven.

That experience at such a young age was the first of several times in my life when I witnessed the ignorance of others and saw the destructive effects of man's behaviour towards animals.

Algerian War of Independence 1956

Algeria was one of France's overseas territories and became a destination for thousands of European immigrants. However, the indigenous Muslims who remained a majority of the territory's population were regarded by the French as an inferior underclass that had to be tightly controlled. This and other factors gave rise to the Algerian nationalist movement which emerged between World War I and World War II to demand equal rights. France resisted giving Muslims such rights and resentment for the French government grew. By the 1950s, revolutionaries within the Algerian nationalist movement were being forced into exile or hiding.

In 1954 Ahmed Ben Bella, a former sergeant in the French Army, collaborated with eight other Algerian exiles in Egypt to set up a revolutionary committee with the aim of gaining independence for Algeria. The group, which became known as the National Liberation Front (*Front de Libération Nationale, FLN*), steadily grew and launched coordinated attacks on public buildings, military and police posts and communication centres. France responded by sending 4,000 troops to try and quell the uprising, resulting in widespread rumours of

1956. Algeria. Having tea with French allies during the war in Algeria.

Credit: RdeT collection

1956. Algeria. A temporary resting place during the war in Algeria.

Credit: RdeT collection

1956. Algeria. During field training in preparation for any surprise attacks.

Credit: RdeT collection

brutality and torture, mass executions and concentration camps. World opinion began to rapidly turn against France.

When I was staying in Washington, the war in Algeria was a topic of conversation at dinner parties I attended, as many invited guests were either involved or interested in politics. It was assumed that I knew what was happening in Algeria, but of course I only knew what I read in the newspapers, yet repeatedly I was asked questions about the reports of torture and extreme violence. There was also conflicting information circulating from the report of an American observer who had been sent to Algeria by the United States government, as it was unclear from his report whether the war was coming to an end or accelerating.

I promised my hosts in Washington that I would speak to friends in the political field as soon as I returned to Paris and send them up-to-date details. So I did exactly as promised, but was astounded when a high-ranking military official invited me to go to Algeria as a 'reporter' so I could eventually give my personal report to my contacts in the USA. Although my visit was not an 'official' visit, all arrangements were made for me by a government official. What an opportunity for me, not just to travel but also to experience an entirely new situation: Algeria fighting for its independence from France. I was excited, although apprehensive.

Extracts from my original report, 1956:

> After spending a few days in Paris listening to people telling me I was crazy, that I would not come back alive, that Algeria was no place for women, I got my papers and *ordre de mission*. The big day came and I was off on the night train to Marseille where I was to board a naval plane. I was the only woman on board which caused some surprise ... and suspicion.
>
> We landed in Oran, an ancient town with Spanish influence from the sixteenth and seventeenth centuries. It was so dark and the atmosphere at the airport was dismal, just a few lights shaking in the wind and a big searchlight turning round and round. We climbed into a rickety bus and lurched along the road which in

some places had been washed away by the rain and in others destroyed by the rebels. There was a newspaper on the seat next to me and I glanced at the advertisement which read: '*Have you got your bullet proof vest? Buy it today, don't wait until tomorrow*'. What might happen tomorrow, I wondered.

We continued on to the navy headquarters at Fort Lamoune where a French Algerian woman was expecting me. She could not understand why I was there, as she had never met a woman reporter before.

It was night-time and dark when I got to my room and I quickly slipped into bed. Suddenly I felt something land on my bed and bounce off: I dared not move. Had someone thrown a bomb into my room? I lay very still and strained my eyes in the darkness to try and see what shape it was. I glanced at the floor beside my bed but all I could see was my suitcase. I slowly reached for the light, holding my breath, in fear that any movement might trigger off the bomb. I slowly switched on the light and saw that opposite my suitcase was a large cupboard. As I raised my eyes to the top half of the cupboard, staring down at me was ... a large cat. What a relief! I had almost convinced myself that I was about to be blown up on my first day in Algeria. The cat had obviously jumped on, then off my bed and taken refuge on the top of the cupboard.

The next morning I was taken to meet Admiral Ponchardier, a strong, heavy, and lively man with a great sense of humour. He had been one of the first people to set foot on a captured pirate ship and he handed me the jersey which had belonged to the pirate captain. It reached down to my knees, but I was very happy to have it as the weather was so cold. I started to ask him questions about the war but he stopped me short with: '*No questions, you are here to find out for yourself. Are you frightened of being killed?*' I assured him I was not. '*That's the sort of girl I like, I will send you on different operations, I don't care if you are killed but I don't want you to ever get in anyone's way during an encounter, no woman has ever been on these sorts of operations, so keep your eyes open.*'

I was sent by convoy one night to a nearby unit along the

Moroccan border. Aymar Achille-Fould, the commanding officer, was a wine grower from the Bordeaux region of France. He had learned that sixty *fellaghas* (rebels with the National Liberation Front) were planning an attack that night so he was preparing his men for a night-time ambush. I asked if I could go along but his first answer was **no**, as I did not have any training for long difficult night marches. However, in response to my pleading, he reluctantly agreed that I could go.

We left a few minutes later, marching in single file with four to five yards between each of us. I soon began to realise how difficult this would be. It was pitch black, my eyes were straining to follow the man ahead of me and we were not walking along a road *but* across Algerian hills of rocks, stones, crevasses with cactus and brush. One minute we were descending, the next going up almost vertically, while moving carefully in complete silence. Every few yards we would halt, drop to one knee and listen for a few minutes before moving on again.

We eventually arrived at a place where two trails coming from Morocco could be watched. My eyes were getting used to the dark and I imagined shadows everywhere, but the only sounds were from dogs and jackals somewhere in the distance. It was so very cold, even though I was wearing four sweaters I felt almost numb, although my mind was clear and alert. On an occasion like this any sound or movement provokes an immediate reaction. I heard a stone rolling and whispered to a companion that I could hear a noise. He whispered back in response: '*Don't be too imaginative.*'

We sat there for more than two hours, but heard nothing other than the usual night sounds of animals. We started back for camp and saw to our horror that some of our men had been ambushed without us knowing – they were still there, half-buried in a haystack with their throats cut.

After we arrived back at camp we were drinking coffee when one of the sentries reported that a white rocket had just been seen. This meant that some of the *fellaghas* had managed to slip through the French lines and were well ahead of us. The rocket was a sign to show their colleagues in Morocco that all had gone well for them.

The following day we traced some footprints which extended about 60 yards from where our men had been ambushed. The rebels had come through without a sound, although the commanding officer said to me: '*You have very good hearing; this is where you heard the rolling stone.*'

From the military base, I travelled around the area for the next two weeks with French military divisions, but was not shielded from the harsh reality of war. I saw numerous acts of torture, dead bodies, women and children terrified fearing what might happen to them. It is well documented in historical records that terrible acts of torture were used by the opposing sides. Such torture included interrogation with a gun held to the head; electric shock treatment; intimidation with threats of execution; allowing prisoners to 'escape' then shooting them as they fled, also other humiliating methods of 'persuasion'. I saw two prisoners tied to each other by having one man's right leg tied to the other man's left leg. They were then told they could run away. The terrified men stumbled away from the soldiers and ran straight into the barbed wire surrounding the area. As they fell to the ground they were shot.

Another time we went to a village where the head man was questioned and was about to be arrested. He hurriedly swallowed something and immediately started frothing at the mouth, then fell to the ground and died: suicide.

In contrast I found it rewarding to be able to travel to rural areas with the military doctors and help with the medical needs of people in the outlying villages. Many had tuberculosis; others had injuries from the bombing and raids. There were people with horrific neck wounds where a distinct shape had been carved across their throats by their compatriots suspecting them of collaborating with the French. My experience as a trainee nurse came in useful and I was able to actively contribute in a practical way, as opposed to just writing notes on my observations. However it was physically demanding as we had to walk for hours to reach some of the villages – no roads, just worn tracks meandering across the rough terrain to the basic homes of the villagers.

On one occasion I was told to rest for a few hours in a

derelict house while the soldiers were attending to other matters. I was suddenly aware of an elderly man in the building. I asked him why he was there and he told me that he had travelled into town with his donkey and cart, and had been stopped and questioned as he was suspected of carrying messages from the local rebels. He was then arrested and tortured. Chains had been attached to his hands, his feet and his testicles and he had been strung up to a beam. He had eventually been taken down and told to wait in the building, so he assumed that the soldiers had realised their mistake and that he was no threat. His hands and feet were grossly swollen and several teeth were missing as a result of his ordeal so I broke some bread into very small pieces, peeled him an orange and helped him to eat. He told me he had a wife and several children who would be wondering why he was away from home for so long. After a short while, the soldiers returned to the building and told the exhausted man to go with them. I asked: *'Are you releasing him?'* The reply was: *'no,'* and almost simultaneously a loud gunshot filled the air. The man fell to the ground.

One evening when staying in Algiers, I was asked by Gae de Viaris, a French civilian, if I would accompany him on an unofficial mission. He lived in Algeria and helped the military negotiate with the opposing rebels. He told me to be smartly dressed, as a sign of respect for the chief we would be meeting, so not knowing where we were going, I wore my new high-heeled shoes, recently purchased in the USA.

We drove about 60 kilometres from Algiers and slowly moved into an isolated area. After a few minutes a light flashed three times as a signal and a man appeared alongside our car. I was politely asked to get out of the car and follow him, so quietly I cooperated and was led to a tree where I was told to remain until instructed to move. It was very dark without even any light from the moon and the tree was standing in an area which was muddy and rocky, so my high-heeled shoes were not exactly the best footwear for such an occasion!

Gae was led away to meet the chief and I stood motionless against the tree as instructed. I could hear soldiers from the

French Army idly chattering as they walked along the road close by, quite oblivious to me standing just a few feet away from them. After about fifteen minutes, I heard a low coughing sound, then another, then another and I realised that I had not been alone but was being watched from the surrounding trees and now after testing my reactions, the rebels were letting me know they were there.

Suddenly a man appeared out of the darkness and instructed me to follow him to a hut nearby where Gae and the chief were in deep conversation. I was led inside the hut but as I went in, Gae and the chief broke off their discussion and went outside. The door was closed behind me and I was on my own in the dimly-lit hut, with only the light from a candle on a shelf. My eyes darted around the room and I saw a machine gun close to the fireplace. I knew there were likely to be identification numbers stamped on the gun, specific to the country of manufacture, so I carefully took the candle from the shelf and held it close to the gun, in an attempt to try and see any marks. I managed to find the numbers and concentrated hard to memorise them. I had memorised just a few numbers, my eyes straining in the dim candlelight, when I heard some steps approaching the hut. I hurriedly tried to put the candle back on the shelf but it would not stick. As Gae and the chief came in, I grabbed the candle and pretended I was warming my hands.

Gae had to leave the hut again, but the chief stayed with me until he returned some two hours later. The chief did not appear to be an extremist, and he explained their side of the struggle to me. As we drove away from the area, the conversation between the chief and me was echoing in my mind. Somehow I felt humbled to have learnt so much about the opposing side, their views and their grievances. The old adage kept reverberating in my head ... there are always two sides to every story.

Many of the Arabs were loyal to France and had studied and worked in France for several years to earn money to buy land for their families back home. I talked to one such man and his brother for some time and they gave me their thoughts and opinions on the war. One of the brothers was actively involved in rallying the Arabs to support France and oppose the rebels, but because of this they were looked on with suspicion and were constantly on their guard against attacks.

This story has a sad ending: the day after our conversation, the brother who had been actively rallying support for France, was brutally murdered in broad daylight in a public place. He was killed with a kitchen knife outside the local shops and his body was thrown into a stream, but nobody admitted to having seen or heard anything. I was so upset. Was he killed because he had been seen speaking with me?

Being a woman, I was not allowed to attend the funeral, and could only watch from a distance. He was carried from his house draped in a sheet, lying on a stretcher and taken to his tomb. His two wives, his mother, mothers-in-law, sisters and other women in the family were outside their house screaming, scratching their faces, moaning in anguish as they stretched out their hands trying to touch him for the last time.

A few days later his brother came to the headquarters and said that he wanted to take on his brother's role of rallying the Arabs to support the French against the rebels. He also said that the people responsible for his brother's death had been rounded up and killed, at the exact same place where his brother was killed.

I visited a school in the town, a modern building. Some 95% of the students' parents were illiterate but they all wanted their children to learn how to read and write, although the *FLN* is opposed to Arab children being educated by the French. I also visited a hospital, another modern place, where most of the children looked healthy, but their parents did not want them to go home as it was safer for them to stay at the hospital.

It will be a long time before women in this part of the world get some sort of emancipation; they are regarded as inferior beings and are made to work and bear children. One lady came to the hospital and said she could not have children. The doctor examined her and said ... *'but you have had children.'* *'Oh yes,'* she replied, *'I have nine but I can't seem to have any more, it is so sad, please cure me.'*

How often I have seen men sitting idly in the sun while their wives carry heavy jars of water on their heads; not one man will move to help even the oldest woman who can hardly put one foot in front of the other. On market days, men ride their donkeys and women follow carrying extra bundles, but since the hostilities began, women are made to walk ahead of the men just in case there is a mine on the path. However, in larger towns, the situation is said to be slowly changing. Many Arabs have seen how Europeans live and how they respect women, so this is starting to create a positive impression.

Just before I left Algeria I was so annoyed to see some French infantry airmen letting their police dogs loose on Arab children. Although the dogs were muzzled, the children were terribly frightened. I told the airmen in strong terms what I thought of them and their disgusting behaviour and then I went in search of the children to give them some sweets. This made the children very happy and they followed me, trying to convince me that the dogs had torn their clothes, but of course this was not true!

I was back in Paris twenty-four hours later. I felt very disturbed about the scenes I had seen and had haunting flashbacks of the terrified families and children caught up in the war. I decided to offer my help to a school in Paris for Algerian children who had fled to France with their families. *Pères Blancs*, the Catholic order managing the school, asked me if I would teach the children to speak French, so I worked as a volunteer-teacher for about a year and loved helping the children to integrate into the French way of life. My experiences in Algeria certainly helped me to understand some of the traumas the children and their parents had faced in their homeland.

In March 1962 a ceasefire was negotiated between the French and the *FLN* with a referendum in July. The Algerian people voted for independence and Algeria was declared an independent country on 3 July 1962. Even though I had been in Algeria for a relatively short period, I had seen and heard enough to convince me that the differences in culture and beliefs were perceived by both sides to be an overwhelming barrier to integration, so I was not surprised that the voting was in favour of independence from France.

Hungarian Uprising, 1956

Josef Stalin, leader of the Soviet Union, died in 1953. He had ruled over the communist countries of the Soviet Union with tight control for almost thirty years, but now his death signalled hopes of new reforms for these countries.

There was growing unrest in Eastern Europe in protest at the Soviet Union occupation. On 23 October 1956, students in Hungary gathered at the Bem Statue to lay a wreath, as a symbol of solidarity with pro-reform movements in Poland. The statue of Polish-born General Bem was a famous landmark in Budapest and was a memorial to the popular general who had led the Hungarian liberation fight of 1848–49 against the Austrian Habsburg Empire. Hungarian patriotic songs were sung and the communist flag was torn down. The crowd grew to some 20,000 strong and together they marched to the Hungarian Parliament to demand the withdrawal of Soviet troops, and to demand independence from the Soviet bloc.

What began as a peaceful demonstration became a full-scale riot when the security police opened fire on the crowds in an attempt to disperse them. The following day, Soviet tanks moved into Budapest as the battles continued, with the escalating unrest also spreading to the rural areas. Senior government officials fled to the Soviet Union and the government collapsed.

A new government was installed and the fighting appeared to subside. However on 4 November more Soviet tanks arrived in Hungary and brutally crushed the uprising. An estimated 2,500 people died, 13,000 were injured, and 200,000 people fled to Western European countries as refugees.

In December 1956, I was invited to Austria, to attend the wedding of Archduchess Maria Ileana of Austria and Count Jaroslav Kottulinsky, in Vienna. After the beautiful, fairy-tale wedding, I contacted the French Ambassador in Hungary, Jean Paul-Boncour and his wife Mausi. They were close friends of mine and on hearing that I was in a neighbouring country, they invited me to stay with them in Budapest.

It was just a month after the Soviet tanks had crushed the uprising and as soon as I arrived in Hungary I could sense the atmosphere of unease. The wedding in Vienna had been such a joyous occasion, but the sights on the streets of Budapest were far from joyous, with so many of the beautiful, old buildings bearing the scars and battle wounds of the indiscriminate firing. There seemed to be beggars everywhere.

I went with Mausi to a shop which had practically no goods to sell and as we came out I was so saddened to see a dignified old man, begging. We immediately gave him some money and as he thanked us he said in French: '*France is such a beautiful country...*' Clearly, he appeared to be an educated man as he had understood our conversation in French and responded in a cultured accent. However, war does not discriminate and anyone regardless of his status in life can find himself lost, bewildered and desperate.

The French embassy helped many people (unofficially, of course) and got them to safety. They also provided packages of essential food supplies which they distributed secretly. So many Hungarians had lost their homes; many families had suffered through loved ones being killed or injured, and some people had simply fled the country in desperation, leaving behind family members.

Many individuals seen by the communist regime as political threats were held in undisclosed prisons, so their families didn't know if they were dead or alive. Everywhere there was sadness, suspicion and despair. Rumours of secret executions were rife, with fears of deportation to the Soviet Union. On so many occasions in my life I've seen at first hand just what the word freedom means and how precious it is to our very existence. I have also seen how futile war appears to be for so many innocent bystanders.

The people of Hungary were suppressed and dominated by the Soviet Union for almost forty years, but in 1989 the 'Iron Curtain' came down as communism collapsed and the people were free. I watched TV at my home in France with emotion and elation, as scenes of such happiness and hope spread around the streets of Hungary, with people openly shedding tears of joy. I remembered the tortured faces of the people I'd seen in 1956, some thirty years before, and I too shed tears of happiness for the people of Hungary, as they could now enjoy their freedom – the basic right for all human-kind.

Earthquake in Iran 1962

At a dinner party in Paris I met some people who owned a Lebanese airline and by the end of the evening they had given me an airline ticket to visit Beirut. So in 1962, I set off for a visit to Lebanon. What a warm welcome was waiting for me, with days of non-stop parties to celebrate my arrival, but horror of horrors, the delicacies I was offered included the heads of little songbirds: a 'delicious' snack in Lebanon. Although my hosts were so accommodating and the house was luxurious, I could not bear to see the poor little birds in tiny cages waiting to be eaten.

After a few days in Beirut, I contacted Hossein and Mosein Garagoslu, my friends in Persia (as Iran was more commonly known then) and arranged to fly to Tehran where Hossein was a minister at the court of the Shah. On arrival at their grand home I rested, then prepared for a dinner party that was being given in my honour at the home of the director of Coca Cola. Before leaving we had an aperitif.

As we were driving to the dinner party I saw people rushing around, some wearing their nightclothes. Strangely, birds were swooping up and down in uncoordinated flight, most unusual, especially as it was dark. On arriving at our destination I was greeted warmly as we waited for other guests to arrive. A few minutes later as I sat on the sofa, I felt a giddy feeling come over me. The room started to spin and I thought, but *it's not possible, how can I be drunk? I've only had a few sips of vodka and some caviar.* The light fittings started to sway and water splashed over the edge of the swimming pool. The director of Coca Cola said just one word: 'Earthquake!' We had not felt the telltale signs in the moving car, but it explained why people were behaving strangely in the streets, rushing around in their pyjamas.

The earthquake struck Boein-Zahra, Qazvin, in north west Iran, some 120 kilometres north of Tehran. It was powerful, measuring 6.9 on the Richter scale with the effects felt in Tehran and surrounding areas. Some 300 villages were destroyed and more than 12,000 people were killed.

There was an immediate response to the disaster with international aid promised by America and France. Also American medical troops stationed in Weisbaden, south west Germany, arrived within a few days to set up a hospital. As I spoke both English and French fluently, I immediately offered to help as an interpreter and persuaded my hosts to allow me to go with the American troops to the edge of the earthquake area, where they were setting up their field hospital.

There were hundreds of wounded people waiting at the temporary hospital, many with severe burns from kerosene lamps which had fallen on them during the earthquake. Also some of the village homes had literally gone up in flames before the occupants could escape, resulting in horrendous burns. One lady had most of the flesh burned off her face and body, her badly-burnt eyes protruding from their sockets.

There was no available water supply, so large water tankers were brought into the area to provide water for both humans and farm animals, but on the day of the Shah's visit, the water was used to settle the dust on the roads.

Every day for about a month I worked at the hospital, my training as a nurse in Paris and my language skills proving so useful. I also went out in the helicopters searching for injured people. An American army colonel ran the hospital most efficiently, but often drugs and bandages were stolen; even blankets and tents 'went missing'. The colonel, a warm, kindly man, turned a blind eye although he was well aware of what was happening. He told me that he had been a prisoner of war in Vietnam and had also learned to steal when he and his companions were desperate for food. He described how they stole chickens by luring them with crumbs attached to pieces of string and patiently reeling them in until they could grab them.

It was a difficult time in Iran as there was political unrest as well as the earthquake tragedy. I met the Shah of Persia briefly, also the Empress, but it was not the time for unnecessary meetings. However I did get the chance to see some beautiful museums, and also went to Persepolis to see the ancient UNESCO World Heritage Site dating back to 515 BC and to Shiraz, capital of the Fars province in south west Iran, said to be one of the most beautiful historical cities in the world.

I was invited to the palatial home of the Shah's sister and her husband, the Minister of Fine Arts. The house was breathtaking with a waterfall cascading from an upper floor alongside the sweeping staircase. There was a romantic aura as beautiful white streamlined cats roamed freely and majestically around the house and grounds. Aides dressed in long, flowing robes moved silently making sure that everyone was personally attended to; there was even a man reciting poetry.

I eventually returned to France feeling thankful that I had been able to help in some small way with the disaster, but I also felt a sense of guilt as I was able to escape from the situation, whereas others were not so fortunate. So many people were so badly burned, scarred and traumatised for the rest of their lives. Almost every family within a wide radius of the earthquake area had lost loved ones or were victims, affected in various ways as a direct result of the earthquake. Once again my father's words came into my mind: *always remember you were born to a privileged life ... so many are not so fortunate but should be helped whenever possible.*

War in Nigeria: Biafra 1969

Nigeria gained independence from Britain in 1960 and a federation, with a federal constitution, was created. There were more than 300 different ethnic and cultural groups in Nigeria, with the Hausa and Fulani living mainly in the north; the Yoruba in the south-west and the Ibo in the south-east. Unfortunately, for a number of complex reasons, there was growing unrest amongst different political parties and ethnic groups, which was largely exacerbated by the way in which the boundaries of former colonies had been defined; not according to ethnicity, but competing claims of colonial powers. As a result, by the mid-1960s, Nigeria was made up of semi-autonomous Muslim feudal states in the northern desert areas, with Christian and animist populations in the south and east – the areas where oil, Nigeria's source of income was exploited.

As ethnic tension increased, the economic situation declined and the military took over the running of the country, as civil war took hold. About 30,000 Ibo were killed almost overnight in Lagos while fighting with the Hausas and a reported 1 million Ibo refugees fled to their homeland in the east.

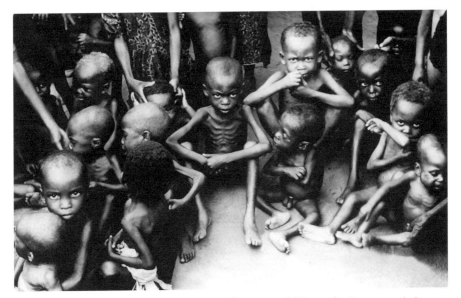

1969. Biafra, Nigeria. A typical scene of starving children, the innocent victims of the war.

Credit: Comité d'Action pour le Biafra, 18 Avenue de Friedland 18 75-PARIS

In May 1967, the head of the eastern region, General Emeka Ojukwu broke away from federal rule and declared the eastern area as the independent Republic of Biafra. At first their military efforts appeared to be winning what would be called the Nigerian Civil War, but within two years 1 million Biafran civilians had died from warfare, disease or starvation.

I joined an action group in Paris that was trying to find ways of providing aid for Biafra. The group was called *Comité d'Action pour le Biafra* (*CAB*) and worked with the Biafra delegation in France. The *CAB* wanted to make a film of the situation on the ground, so they asked me if I would be prepared to go to Biafra to document the extent of the atrocities.

I asked Maurice Schumann, French Minister of Foreign Affairs, for his opinion and he agreed that I should go to Biafra and report back to him and he quickly arranged for my travel and stay in Libreville, a former French colony. I was met by staff from the charity, the Order of Malta, and stayed at the home of Marina Vlady, an actress married at the time to a French pilot. I spent a few days in Libreville

89

1969. Biafra, Nigeria. With Madame Nijoleka Ojukwu, wife of General Ojukwu.

Credit: Comité d'Action pour le Biafra, 18 Avenue de Friedland 18 75-PARIS

with contacts, learning about the situation and developments in Biafra and on 19 November 1969, I set off in a small Red Cross plane with just the pilot and a nurse on board, plus medical supplies and a consignment of salt.

Extracts from my Biafra diary as documented in November 1969:

19 November 1969

When the pilot was coming in to land on the small airstrip in a field, he had to close down the lights on the plane and try to land in darkness, as the 'intruder' plane from the opposing military was hovering above us. The intruder was waiting to bomb any aircraft arriving in Biafra to prevent much needed supplies and foreign aid coming into the area. We had to hold

90

back for a couple of hours before trying to land in the darkness, but suddenly we were spotted by the intruder and immediately our plane was bombed! The force of the bombing caused our small aircraft to hurtle through the night sky, engulfed in flames. As we started to fall, the force of the plane spinning miraculously put out the flames just as we plunged to the ground.

The skilful pilot somehow kept control as it spun round and round and even with a crash landing, he got us safely on the ground: it was indeed a dramatic entry into Biafra. There were so many people waiting for us, watching the unfolding drama and ready to help – the French Red Cross, the Irish Sisters, Father McNulty, other aid workers and local people – but as the flames were already out, the local people produced basins, as if by magic, and collected the fuel dripping out of the plane. Strangely, I felt calm and composed as I walked down the steps of the plane and was greeted by so many people.

Mr Ryst, representative for the French Red Cross, told the local people who were helping to unload the plane that a sack of salt would be distributed amongst them if the cargo was unloaded in fifteen minutes. There was wild activity as people scurried back and forth, frantically trying to claim their share of the reward. Two sacks of rice split open and everyone carefully scraped up the grains of rice – amazingly, they all seemed to carry bags in their pockets. They even swept the floor of the plane after unloading and swept outside on the airstrip, carefully retrieving any precious remains of salt that had seeped through the sacks, or any stray grains of rice. And all this was done in fifteen minutes by the dim light of pocket torches!

There were ten children waiting for our plane to land as it was scheduled to take them to the hospital in Libreville run by the Red Cross and the Order of Malta, but of course this was not possible as the plane had seventeen holes in the fuselage. The poor children were exhausted, waiting at this late hour, many seriously ill with conditions such as tuberculosis and malnutrition. I gave them some lollipops, but a child whose head was misshapen through the effects of cancer, did not have the energy to suck his. My heart cried out in anguish for these innocent children. Fortunately a plane from Belgium was expected and would take them to Libreville.

Mr Ryst took me and my luggage to the customs post, but before leaving the 'airfield' we came to the roadblocks where men were stationed with bayonets and guns. As soon as they saw the Red Cross identification papers, they quickly stepped aside and waved us on our way, especially as the chief of protocol, Mr Unachutw was also in the car escorting me to the State House, a journey of about 50 km. As we were driving, my narrow escape from death suddenly hit me and panic engulfed my senses as I relived the experience of the plane catching fire. Fortunately, I was able to quickly recover and shrug off the unnerving sensation.

We travelled through the lush vegetation of the jungle, with a few huts dotted sparsely amongst the clearings and eventually reached our destination. I was shown to my room; there was a clean bed, a candle and a pail of water in the wash area. There was no electricity and the window panes were painted a muddy blue-green colour for camouflage. In a neighbouring room Mr Burke from Canadian Television and Major Hamilton from Britain were preparing to leave Biafra. I gave Major Hamilton letters to post for my family and for Maurice Schumann, saying that I had arrived safely, not mentioning of course our hazardous entry into Biafra, just a few hours earlier.

20 November

I met the Permanent Secretary for Foreign Affairs and visited the Red Cross International Centre where two Swiss nurses and a Spanish doctor were working round the clock. They were treating twenty seriously wounded young men aged between about 18 and 20, who had injuries such as broken legs and shrapnel buried deep in their bodies. Some were shell-shocked, obviously dazed and totally disorientated from the noise and trauma of gunfire and fear. One young man was waiting to have a leg amputated and just sat silently staring into space. A father was anxiously watching his severely injured children, his wife already dead beside him.

In the evening I met the Minister of Justice and shared a welcome meal of corned beef and cauliflower. Philip Effiong, head of navy, aviation and land was there and I asked if I could go to the front to witness the fighting and he agreed to take me. Dr Kookey, commissioner for special duties and province administrator for Opobo, was also there, arranging for children to be evacuated to Europe.

21 November

Visited the teaching hospital where Professor Udekwu was working day and night. It was a modern building compared to other places in the area, but there was a great shortage of medical supplies. The professor had worked for fourteen years in the USA and had formed a group there to support Biafra, providing medication, equipment and funding but now there were more than 600 patients at the hospital, mainly wounded soldiers. In addition 300 people came to the outpatient clinic, which was held three times a week. Many seeking medical help walked there from up to 20 kilometres away, so many women carrying children … just skeletons … many people with tuberculosis.

In the maternity unit women were giving birth; many babies were born prematurely, their mothers malnourished. So many of the new-born babies resembled misshapen dolls with no flesh and many of the mothers lifted their babies up to the cameras to show the awful misery of the situation.

We moved on to another centre run by the Irish nuns, supported by Caritas, the international Catholic relief agency. Their building was well equipped and nourishing food such as fruit and milk was available, so security guards were on duty to deter the regular break-ins from desperate people trying to feed their families. The sick and wounded were given nutritious food and were lying on bedframes, mattresses or mats. There were no blankets, some had no clothes, others were wrapped in rags, and a dead body was rolled up in an old carpet. It was so very hot and the stench of urine, blood and gangrene was overpowering. There were no toilets, just a tin can. I watched the surgeon as he skilfully removed bullets from a badly-wounded soldier.

In contrast, others who appeared to be recovering were making woven cane baskets and I was given one; I will treasure it. I went with the chief nurse from ward to ward and gave out cigarettes, which was all I had to give. How I wished I had brought something more useful, something that was desperately needed. The patients and the staff started clapping and cried out: '*Welcome, welcome to Biafra, thank you France.*' I was overcome with emotion but fortunately there was an amusing moment to ease my tension when the chief nurse introduced me as Princess de Gaulle!

22 November

Went to Owerri to see the caring work of the Irish priests. It was a hazardous journey as the intruder planes were hovering in the area ready to bomb any vehicles they spotted. The driver drove so fast, dashing under trees every few minutes to avoid detection.

I visited a sick bay in Obibi where there were 140 children in one room, their mattresses lined up in a row. There were numerous old men and women in various stages of life; many close to death. One lady who was in better health than most of the others, suddenly got up and acted out my arrival in Biafra, demonstrating how the plane caught fire and how it landed. How did she know? A good example of the 'bush telegraph'.

I took clothes to the refugee camp, but wished I had taken salt as it was so desperately needed. However a dress given to me by a relative was soon being modelled by one of the refugees. She was so thrilled with it, little did she realise it had come from a princess, from a castle in Belgium. I smiled at her thinking she looked far more beautiful wearing the dress than my relative had looked!

23 November

Visited a hospital run by Swiss doctors and nurses. At a meeting to discuss patients' treatments, I heard that a soldier in the hospital was close to death as he needed a blood transfusion, but there was no A negative blood available, as it was an uncommon blood type in Biafra. *'But that is my blood group,'* I exclaimed, *'please take some and give it to him.'* I was so happy that he survived and later received a message to say that he was eventually able to leave the hospital and had rejoined his unit.

24 November

Travelled to Emekuku feeding centre where 860 old people came to eat a small meal – no more than a handful of rice. Later I met General Ojukwu, followed by a press conference. I was asked my opinion of the situation. I tried to explain how I felt about my experiences of the last few days, visiting the hospitals and centres where so few were desperately trying to save the lives of so many. But alas, I could not utter one word, as the horrific sights and reality of the situation suddenly hit me. I felt hot, wet tears on my cheeks and I was totally overwhelmed as images of starving children, dying and dead babies in their mothers' arms, desperate parents, severely-wounded soldiers and bewildered old people came flooding into my mind. I was overcome with sadness, a profound feeling of uselessness – I felt paralysed and unable to continue with the interview. In the evening I spent a couple of hours at General Ojukwu's house and having regained my composure was able to speak freely with his wife Njiuleka Ojukwu and describe what I had seen.

25 November

Met Professor Bede Okigbo, coordinator of the Land Army Programme, set up to combat the terrible famine in Biafra. He had recently travelled to Israel to learn how to grow a high protein root crop; how to rear fast growing carp and poultry; how to raise a small breed of cow and how to turn bushland into fertile farmland. Each town and village had set up a division and a sub-division for the programme.

On the way to the rehabilitation centre in Ikeona we were caught up in an air-raid and had to hide as I was wearing a white dress – very foolish as easily spotted! The centre was very busy teaching war invalids, orphans and refugees how to fish and work on the land. Others were learning how to sew, but there was a desperate shortage of needles, cloth and sewing machines.

26 November

Today I visited a centre run by Mother Ursula and some Irish nuns who are in charge of fifteen feeding centres, providing food for 4,000 children every day. The children walk for miles in the dark to come to the centre for food consisting of a bowl of thin porridge or gruel. Then they walk home again before dawn so that they are not spotted. Before the meal, the children sang to give thanks for the food and it was such a moving experience to see and hear these thin and undernourished children singing – many of them seemed to be little more than babies. It's a sight I will never forget.

I returned to my room to change into camouflage dress as General Effiong was taking me to a guerrilla training camp, a hideout deep in the bush where 200 men and women lived and trained. I was immediately struck with the beauty of one of the guerrillas, Veronica, who I was told had been an Olympic athlete before the war. She showed me how they trained to creep up on the enemy silently and steal their weapons while they slept.

However my visit to the fighting front had to be abandoned as there was a bombing attack just a few hours before I was due to visit and the area was too dangerous to enter.

I had another task to complete before leaving Biafra, on behalf of my friend Baroness von Oppenheim. Her husband Christian, Baron von Oppenheim, a German banker, was flying on business in October 1967 when his plane crashed near Lagos and he was killed. The family lawyers had been trying for two years to get a death certificate as they needed it for insurance purposes and other legal matters, but had been unsuccessful, so the Oppenheim family asked me if I would try to penetrate the 'red tape' while in Biafra and act on their behalf. It was a difficult and frustrating task, but I was relieved when the death certificate was issued just before I left Biafra, so I was able to take the documents home for the family. The cause of the plane crash has never been verified and still remains a mystery.

My return journey to France was also eventful. Two planes were due to arrive from Libreville, a Belgian plane and a French one. When they eventually landed, the French Red Cross plane had again been hit by bombs from the intruder plane, but fortunately the Belgian plane arrived unscathed. Most of the departing aid workers opted to travel to their various destinations on the Belgian plane, but I chose to travel with the French pilot as he was same pilot who had skilfully secured my safe arrival in Biafra. Once in the air, I dreamed of eating a yoghurt in Paris.

Following my return to France, I no longer seemed to enjoy the grand dinners and parties as I had in the past. I had lost my appetite because of the extreme hunger and starvation I had seen. How unfair that so many innocent adults and children lived in poverty, desperation and extreme hunger – their goal was just to survive – while so many of us, by comparison, had so much. Most of us have absolutely no concept of what it would be like to die slowly of starvation and watch helplessly as our children died before our eyes. I had returned to France a different person, with a different agenda in life. My life could never be one long party again.

I reported to Maurice Schumann that in my opinion the war was coming to an end. I felt that it could not continue for much longer as so many had died during its four years– surely there must be a limit to human suffering? The soldiers were weary and the civilians were dying of starvation, so I was not surprised when the war ended in 1970, just a few weeks after my visit. Seeing so many starving,

5

Road to the Refuge

I have often been asked why I've never married. Well, I have been fortunate to know several charming and eligible suitors and indeed there have been opportunities of marriage, but I was always reluctant to make the commitment. Of course my mother had mentally planned for all her seven daughters to be married and to live out their lives happily as grand ladies. She prepared me by declaring that when I married, I must do exactly what my husband told me to do. That was not what I had in mind for my future: after fighting so hard for my independence and living through years of disapproval from some of my family, marriage seemed a step too far; losing my independence seemed too high a price to pay.

I did have a wonderful relationship with a distant cousin, Prince Konstantin of Bavaria. We were the very best of friends, completely in tune mentally – not a deep love affair in the true sense, but certainly we shared common views and opinions and both had a great zeal for life and for adventure. Konstantin was a German politician and we stayed close friends over the years, as I was also active in political circles.

The last time I saw him was in 1969, when I went with him to the airport to wave him bon voyage, as he was returning to Germany. I remember it vividly as I suddenly felt a strange feeling of apprehension and somehow I knew that I would not see him again. Not long afterwards, he was killed over Germany in an aircraft accident, when his plane hit some trees. Konstantin was a true friend, a kindred spirit and a positive influence in my life.

I have often been asked if I have any regrets in life. Surely it is impossible to live almost ninety years without feeling some sadness or disappointment with certain situations. Certainly when thinking

99

of the relationship between me and my mother, I do feel some sadness and regret, as we never achieved a close bond or mutual understanding.

Sadly, I know I was a great disappointment to her in some ways as I rebelled against the closed, almost monastic environment of life at the château and my adventurous nature did not fit my mother's vision of an aristocratic future for her eldest child. We clashed on many occasions. For many years there was an unspoken air of disapproval from several members of my immediate family towards me. How I wish that the situation had been different. What would now be regarded by most parents as quite normal – a child with an independent, enquiring mind, which appeared to be my main 'failing' – was somehow seen by my mother as shameful.

She was a kind, most dignified lady, but did good deeds out of a sense of duty, following her Catholic doctrine almost to the letter, whereas my father, who also had a strong sense of duty, tailored his actions to what he felt was the right thing to do, not through any religious scruples.

On reflection I am sure my mother did all she could to provide me and my siblings with strong moral guidance and a sense of duty. However, to her way of thinking, duty was all about respect and honouring family traditions and keeping up appearances while keeping strictly within the boundaries of one's social class. Duty for my mother also included helping others and when our last nanny retired, a loyal, very English lady named Alice Mabel Pack, she was given a home by my parents. When she died she was buried in my mother's family vault at the church in St Benin d'Azy.

Trying to rationalise my relationship with my mother leads me to believe that I was simply born too soon. If I had been born fifty years later, my thinking and actions would not be seen as wayward or rebellious, but I was born during the cautious years following World War I, not the permissive era of the 1970s. I wish now that I had been able to follow a professional career path, but such an education was rare amongst girls from a background such as mine. Instead my education focused largely on cultural and social attributes such as learning to converse in different languages, classical music and most importantly, etiquette. Knowing how to make a deep curtsey to the Queen, how to curtsey not quite so deeply to a duchess and how *not* to use your hands while speaking, were considered to be necessities for well brought up young ladies.

My father was a cultured, dignified yet very modest man, with a quiet unassuming manner and always ready to help others. He drilled into his children that we must never be boastful, but should do kind deeds quietly, at every opportunity. One day, as a young man, he was late home for dinner and his parents wondered what was keeping him. He eventually arrived, apologised for being late, changed his clothes and then ate his meal. The following day a man came to the door and asked if a young man answering to a certain description lived there.

My grandmother was called to the door by the servant who anticipated a problem, so grandmother spoke to the caller informing him that there *was* a young man living there who fitted the description, her son Léopold, but how could she help? The caller explained that the previous day Léopold had saved the life of his drowning son and he had called to thank him. It was typical of my father to do what was needed, but not to boast of what he did.

My father was forty-four when I was born and was working as a royal envoy. He was already an experienced soldier, having volunteered for service during World War I and fought on the Western Front in the trenches at Ypres, Belgium and survived the terrible battles around the town of Dixmude. But many thousands of soldiers on opposing sides lost their lives. In October 1914, to halt the advance of the Germans, the dykes were opened up which flooded the land and most of the wounded men and animals were drowned, but my father was one of the fortunate soldiers who eventually returned home.

He was kind to all his children and we knew that he loved us unconditionally, but it was not like family life enjoyed by youngsters today. He was away from home a lot and children had their place in life – to be seen, but not heard, so as children we didn't get to know our parents on a one-to-one basis and it would have been unheard of to discuss freely our fears and phobias with them.

I recall an occasion when my father took me to our stables where the beloved family dog, Bendor, a Scottish deerhound, was lying in the straw. Bendor was not moving and as I touched him, I recoiled in dismay as he was rigid and cold, then I threw myself on him, willing him to lift his head and lick my cheek. But I realised that

Tenouches

12 Dec 1933

My darling Betty

Tomorrow is your birthday and I send you all my best best wishes. I am very sorry that I can't be there with you. You have been twelve long years in the world and you have grown from a little tiny baby into a big big girl, almost into a little woman. All these years your mother and I have been loving you and caring for you to the best of our ability. You learnt to walk, to speak, almost to think with someone watching you all the time. Now the time has come for you to begin to act for yourself, and all your life will depend on the way you govern yourself. Now I want to

1933. Letter from my father to me on my 12th birthday.

Credit: RdeT collection

Bendor was dead and that death was cold. I was distraught. I sobbed trying hard to control my emotions, but although my father was sympathetic, I cannot remember him comforting me as a modern day father would almost certainly do in a similar situation – such was life in those days.

102

beg you with all my heart and soul always
to be truthful, constant and strait forward
You have a good affectionate heart but that is
not all, You must be ready to put up with
heardships, and bare with them patiently and
chearfully You have the best mother child ever
had. Do not forget it and try to repay to your best.
Be kind and affectionate to your Grandmother
You will not always have her with you and later
on you will be so glad to remember

We shall soon all be together for Christmas
Pray God that He may keep us all united
in one loving affection for many years to
Come.

a happy happy birthday to you

Your loving Father

1933. Letter from my father to me on my 12th birthday.

Credit: RdeT collection

My father treated staff in a respectful manner and financially helped
nannies and other employees long after their retirement from his
employment. Most of our staff stayed with us for years and Louis
Boutard, a cook, was with us for forty-one years. He had only one
leg and the missing one had been replaced by a wooden one. One

103

day the poor man fell off the toilet and broke his wooden leg!

I often think of my father and invariably I can hear him speaking to me; he was a wonderful example of dignity with humility and I adored him.

Aunt Marie was undoubtedly the greatest influence on my life and I became devoted to her. She was a strong-minded lady with an international way of thinking, never judgemental, always fair and just, with an authoritative air. She loved nature and all creatures, a trait which I seem to have inherited from her. I remember her taking me to Antwerp Zoo when I was about twelve. Even at that young age, I felt uneasy seeing beautiful animals sitting behind bars; somehow it seemed wrong. She too shared these concerns, even though Antwerp Zoo, by zoo standards at the time, was said to be one of the more progressive in the world.

Aunt Marie always had time to listen to me and never lost faith in me during some difficult periods of my life and it was she who actively encouraged me to follow my heart and open an animal refuge. I felt much closer to Aunt Marie than to my mother, as I sensed that she really did understand that I was not exactly rebelling against my heritage, but wanted to explore what the world had to offer and to learn about other cultures and traditions. There was an occasion when I excitedly told my mother that I had been invited to go to India with friends, but she immediately said I could not accept, as our families were not well acquainted. When I told Aunt Marie of the invitation she exclaimed: '*How wonderful, when are you going?*'

Aunt Marie encouraged me to travel and arranged for me to make my first visit to England when I was about twenty. I stayed in Dorset with her friend Rachel de Montmorency, the daughter of Viscount Frankfort de Montmorency. It was the beginning of a lifelong love affair with Britain, the country where I met people who have become some of my greatest friends for the past sixty years, such as Miles Huddlestone, Julian Byng and Freddy and Helia Nicolle. We spent many happy times together at dinner parties at Wrotham Park, Julian's palatial home, also at his London home in St James's Square, where Princess Margaret was also a guest on occasions. I remember having a lively conversation with her at dinner when we discussed our mutual passions: art and ballet.

c.1960. With my dear Aunt Marie, Princess Marie de Croÿ-Solre.

Credit: RdeT collection

Aunt Marie really did open doors for me and I kept up a lively correspondence with her from whichever country I was visiting; she was always so keen to hear what I was doing and where I was going next. All my life I have been prone to bouts of low self-esteem and self-doubt and to this day I feel sick inside and panic if I have to make a presentation or officiate in some way. Possibly knowing of my mother's disapproval and disappointment in me has caused me to react in this way, yet Aunt Marie had the knack of making me feel special and always seemed to boost my confidence.

When Aunt Marie died in June 1968 the following obituary was placed in *The Times* newspaper (24 June 1968) by her friend, the Dowager, Viscountess Falmouth.

PRINCESS M DE CROŸ

Princess Marie de Croÿ whose death was reported on Saturday, will be mourned by many friends old and young, not only in France and Belgium, but in England also.

In World War I she was a leading spirit on the French border in the organisation for helping British soldiers cut off from their comrades after the Battle of Mons. Over 50 years later she is still remembered with gratitude by those who owed her their liberty and often their lives.

During the autumn over 100 officers and men were hidden in or near her château and were equipped with civilian clothes, false papers, and guides to take them safely across Belgium to Holland. Her courage and resource never faltered even when discovery might mean certain death.

On one occasion the German command mounted a surprise search on the château when thirteen men were hidden in the attic. She just had time to hurry them into a blocked-up stairway behind a wall-cupboard and then sat down at her easel to paint, in front of the door. For 2 hours the house was ransacked from attic to cellar, but she never stirred and the searchers left this apparently unconcerned artist, in peace.

Inevitably at last she was detected and spent 4 years in a German prison, only being released when at death's door through the rigours of her confinement. Her steadfastness was an inspiration to her countrymen at the time, and found an echo in the devotion of the resistance in World War II.

From the fateful day of the boar hunt when I was only about eight, I had nursed the idea that one day I would set up an animal shelter and campaign for the protection of all animals and as time went by I knew that this would be my future role in life.

Although I had witnessed the most awful human suffering during my travels, especially in Algeria, Hungary, Persia (Iran), and Biafra, I had met wonderful people doing so much to help, such as the medical teams, the Red Cross and many other charitable organisations, also many other volunteers – all doing whatever they could to ease the pain and trauma of people in distress. But in comparison there seemed to be few people involved with relieving the suffering and abuse of animals, yet I saw evidence of indifference and abuse of animals in every country I visited, sadly also in France.

In December 1965 my father died aged eighty-eight and then in June 1968, my Aunt Marie died at ninety-three. It was a very sad period for me as both my father and my aunt were such special people in my life.

I decided I would continue to assist humanitarian action by supporting the organisations set up to do such work, but personally I would focus on practically trying to relieve animal suffering and would campaign for care and respect for both human and animal lives.

I cannot recall any deliberate intention to give up friends and invitations or opportunities to travel, but over time, one's priorities change. I was now forty-six; it was time to modify my lifestyle.

Life at *Refuge de Thiernay*

By 1968 I already had a sanctuary in the courtyard of a farm belonging to my parents, where there were just six small enclosures for stray dogs. The following year my mother gave me a small farmhouse on the edge of the hamlet of Thiernay and with a very small legacy from

1969. Early days at *Refuge de Thiernay*.

Credit: Gérard Bidolet, 7. Place du Champ de Foire 58 Decize

1969. Early days at *Refuge de Thiernay.*

Credit: Gérard Bidolet, 7. Place du Champ de Foire 58 Decize

Aunt Marie and a donation from a family friend, amounting to around £2000, I bought a piece of land next to the house. This became the home of *Refuge de Thiernay* and a new life began for me.

The house was so basic and somewhat isolated, located at the end of a dirt road which seemed to go nowhere. Friends and acquaintances thought I was crazy to live there as there was no running water; no heating (it was so cold in the winter); no staff; no telephone; no car and I had no money. But I was happy and knew this was meant to be my life from now on. Word spread that I looked after animals, so dogs and cats appeared as if by magic. Dogs arrived in a pitiful condition, some with collar chains embedded in their necks as they had never been taken off since they were puppies and of course the animals had grown.

First of all, I persuaded a friend to make three large enclosures for the dogs; soon afterwards I persuaded him to make another three, making a total of six large enclosures. Albert de Mun, a kind friend of my family, gave me the money for the enclosures as he supported

109

1970. George de Caunes, TV star and animal lover cutting the ribbon
at the Opening of *Refuge de Thiernay*.

Credit: RdeT collection

my view that they must be large, allowing the dogs freedom to play
and behave in a natural manner. I was determined to create large
open spaces for the dogs as I remembered how I had felt and behaved
when confined to a small room during my schooldays. I was so
unhappy at the convent and I certainly did not want the animals to
feel as I had felt – like a frustrated prisoner in a tiny cell.

In 1970, the popular television star, Georges de Caunes, came to
officially open *Refuge de Thiernay* and more than 1,000 people came
to the opening, a huge gathering in such a backwater of France. The
event was widely reported in the media. I was so happy and proud
of my simple Refuge. The following year I registered *Refuge de Thiernay*
as part of my new charity, *Défense et Protection des Animaux*, so I
could then legally accept financial donations and promote the work
of the Refuge.

Having been a 'party girl' for so many years I needed advice,
guidance and direction on how to run an animal shelter and Dr

1987. At Wood Green Animal Shelters, Cambridgeshire with Graham Fuller, Chief Executive Officer.

Credit: WGAS

1994. Entrance to *Refuge de Thiernay.*

Credit: RdeT collection

1994. Typical dog enclosure at *Refuge de Thiernay.*

Credit: RdeT collection

1994. Typical cat enclosure at *Refuge de Thiernay*.

Credit: RdeT collection

1997. Animal Behaviour training session at *Refuge de Thiernay* with Dr Roger Mugford.

Credit: RdeT collection

Constantin Sollogoub, veterinary surgeon in Nevers, became the Refuge veterinarian. He taught me so much about animal diseases, the way to handle animals, how to be observant and recognise their behavioural traits, and how to care for them when they were ill. He became a dear friend (and still is) and also became the vice-president of my charity.

I knew that animal shelters in the UK were far more advanced than in France so I made visits to the RSPCA centres in the UK, became a member society of the International Society for the Protection of Animals (ISPA) and started to attend conferences and training days to increase my understanding of animals. From these sessions I realised that I had a natural instinct and empathy with animals, which indeed boosted my confidence. I learned more from the dedicated people I met and gradually built up a network of people who were never too busy to help and support me. During those early years at the Refuge I desperately needed professional help and it was suggested that I should advertise in the UK veterinary journals for practical help from veterinary nurses, as there was no veterinary nurse training in France, so I was elated when highly-trained British Animal Nursing Association nurses came to my aid and worked in rotation as volunteers. Some of them stayed for several months and some returned in the following years. Iris Baldry from Chelmsford was a wonderful veterinary nurse, physically strong, compassionate, and so practical – we loved her.

In the early 1970s, animal welfare was largely an unknown concept in rural France. Indeed this was the case in most countries throughout the world, especially in rural areas where dogs and cats were kept mainly as watchdogs, sheepdogs, 'ratters' and for other practical purposes. Treatment of these animals was generally harsh and when unable to perform their 'duties', it was common practice to either abandon them or to use a method of disposal such as drowning, or poisoning by feeding them with meatballs laced with strychnine. Even the veterinarians in those days used strychnine to put down animals, which caused a prolonged, painful death.

Life would prove to be an uphill journey at *Refuge de Thiernay* for volunteers and animals and most certainly for me! The numbers of sickly puppies and kittens arriving at the Refuge became a big problem – so many of the dogs were suffering from distemper, a rampant disease at that time; with the cats, most of them semi-wild, suffering from respiratory conditions. Most of these young animals died, which was so depressing for the caring volunteers helping at the Refuge. Also few people in the vicinity of rural Thiernay wanted to adopt an animal, so I had to rely on friends in Paris to help find homes for most of them and arrange annual adoption events there.

At the time local veterinarians did not promote neutering of dogs and cats as their work focused on the care of farm animals. Also they had little interest in cats and dogs, as demand for veterinary treatment for such animals was practically unknown in rural areas. Many country folk thought it was a sin to prevent animals reproducing, also wages were low so why would they want to pay for such operations to be done? Dr Fernand Méry, the founder of the *Conseil National de la Protection Animale*, was the first veterinarian to speak up on this issue in France, stating that vets were not just for cows and pigs, but were there to help all animals.

However, trying to change attitudes on animal birth control was to become a long-term campaign for the *Refuge de Thiernay* and is still very much alive today. I was convinced that controlling animal populations was a key factor for the well-being of animals – so much potential suffering could be prevented. For example, cats and dogs were regularly reproducing unwanted litters, many animals died through disease or malnourishment and many were killed by owners using inhumane methods such as drowning where the animal was first weighed down by a heavy stone tied round its neck. Often such action was taken with great reluctance, but with no known alternative.

In 1971 I discovered that the veterinary school in Lyon had started neutering animals for the general public. I learned this from Dr Chatré (a colleague of Dr Sollogoub) as his son was a veterinary student in Lyon. I arranged to make regular visits to Lyon, taking five or six dogs for neutering on each visit, making a return journey of eight hours in a battered old van! With Pierre Quartier, a wonderful volunteer at the Refuge, we would leave Thiernay at 4 a.m. to reach Lyon in time for the start of the veterinary school's working day. The van had no heating, so plastic bottles were filled with hot water, then wrapped in blankets and placed against the recovering dogs for the return journey to the Refuge.

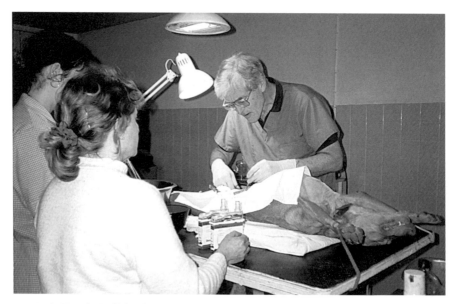

1996. David Griffiths demonstrating a spay operation at the *Refuge de Thiernay* neutering week.

Credit: RdeT collection

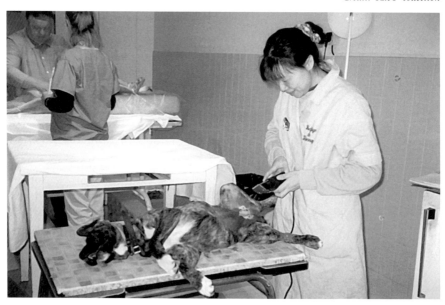

1997. Education week at *Refuge de Thiernay*. Left to right: Dr Pawel Novak (Poland), Kate Fernald (veterinary student from USA), Pei-Feng Su (Taiwan).

Credit: RdeT collection

2000. Josiane Cœuret, Secretary General of *Refuge de Thiernay* and my 'right-hand-woman'.

Credit: RdeT collection

A senior official of the French Veterinary Association told me I was wasting my time and money with neutering, but 20 years later he came to me and said: '*You were right.*' Eventually over time and after negotiating with my local practice, the neutering of cats and dogs became available in my home area, with discounted rates for charities. In addition to neutering, we also promoted vaccination of animals against rabies, distemper and leptospirosis, as being necessary for the animals' health and welfare, as well as to improve public health and hygiene. The *Refuge de Thiernay* was also an early proponent of tattooing for owned animals as a means of identification. This proved invaluable for during just one summer holiday period in France, 6,000 dogs were returned to their owners.

I wanted to learn as much as possible about training dogs to become guide dogs for blind people, so in November 1974 I visited the Guide Dogs for the Blind Association in Leamington, UK, with Monsieur Paul Corteville. Paul had trained eighty guide dogs in France during the previous twenty-five years and was keen to study the methods of training at Leamington and put them into practice in France. Looking back on those early years, I feel proud of the *Refuge de Thiernay*'s efforts even though many people thought I was either eccentric, or more likely, quite mad.

In 1981 ISPA and an organisation called World Federation of Protection Associations amalgamated and became known as the World Society for the Protection of Animals (WSPA). I was invited to become an Advisory Director of WSPA and this title meant that I was a WSPA spokesperson and representative in France. I considered this to be a great honour and I remained an Advisory Director for more than twenty-five years. At the WSPA meetings I met so many like-minded people and was invited to visit organisations in various countries. I tried to copy some of the animal housing I saw in the UK and the USA and used plans and ideas from all the progressive organisations I visited. Although I always regret not having a formal education, as a child I was taught by my nannies to be observant and to memorise as much as I could, so often I would remember something that had caught my eye at a shelter and copy the idea – why not?

I had such a lot of advice from Graham Fuller, Chief Executive Officer of Wood Green Animal Shelters (WGAS) in the 1980s and early 1990s. Graham and his wife Moya, who I met through WSPA, played a vital role in the UK animal welfare movement by creating an animal shelter which was a happy place to visit – aesthetically exciting and futuristic with unusually shaped 'parasol' kennels and large communal enclosures for the dogs. Graham was always looking for new ideas and had the courage and foresight to build a restaurant, an events arena, a wind generator and even a college of animal welfare on the site. His aim was to encourage people to visit the centre with their families, and once on site the animal welfare message became evident through seeing happy, healthy animals, clean and well-maintained facilities, professional trained staff and attractive, informative educational materials.

Historically, animal shelters in so many countries have been depressing places to visit with sad-looking animals staring through the bars in a forlorn manner, but WGAS was built for a new era and the concept has now been adopted or adapted by many other animal welfare charities in the UK and abroad.

I tried to incorporate some of their ideas, such as heated beds for the dogs, chalets for cats, waste disposal units and trees for reducing noise nuisance from barking dogs. I was helped with all of this by Bill Hames, who was recommended by Graham. Bill was a typical well-mannered English gentleman with a charming personality. He was a draughtsman who worked on the WGAS complex in Cambridgeshire and he came to the *Refuge de Thiernay* many times – on one occasion for a week with his delightful wife Mary who transformed my garden. Bill was a realist. He knew that I had little money to make drastic changes to the Refuge, but he gave me ideas for improving the dog kennels and designed simple housing for the cats at a low cost. He taught me that good ideas needn't be expensive, as simple well-planned facilities can be efficient and effective. Sadly, Bill died four years ago and we miss him.

Raising enough funds to meet ongoing expenditure at the Refuge has always been a battle, with fund-raising activities in the early days such as street markets and Christmas parties meeting only part of our needs. But in 1982 the *Refuge de Thiernay* was granted official status (known as Public Utility) with the French government in recognition of services to the community and this meant that in future we would be exempt from paying taxes. Also we could now accept any legacies; our previous status prevented this. In return the Refuge responded by collecting almost every stray animal from the streets, also any animals that were dangerous or causing a public nuisance.

The Refuge continued to grow with the dogs and cats housed on 4 acres and with a further 12 acres for horses and other random farm animals. Now more than twenty-five years later, it has an official contract to provide an animal control service for local authorities, with our remit extended to cover more than three hundred towns and villages. The Refuge now receives payment for this service, a big help for our ever precarious bank balance.

I became well known in veterinary circles as a champion of tattooing, never missing an opportunity to influence the veterinarians' attitudes towards domestic pets; not an easy task as their bread and butter came from farm animals, so their interest in pet animals was limited. But slowly the situation started to change in France as well as in other European countries and in September 1987 I was invited by the Irish Society for the Prevention of Cruelty to Animals, to speak at the Irish Veterinary College in Dublin, on the benefits of tattooing dogs as a means of identification. Then in 1989, almost twenty years after the *Refuge de Thiernay* started tattooing dogs and cats, tattooing became a legal requirement for all owned dogs in France.

Although microchipping is now accepted as the most progressive method of identification, tattooing in my experience is so effective as it is easily visible to anyone who finds a stray animal. Ideally, for greater protection, the animal needs to have a collar with an identity disc attached, a tattoo and a microchip. I recall a few years ago discussing animal tattooing with an official from a dog breeders' club – he was most dismissive of all methods of identification and stated: '*Pedigree dogs don't get lost.*' Really? What a foolish man! Thankfully, responsible and caring breeders do not share his misguided opinion.

Some fourteen years ago, the Refuge introduced a two-week intensive neutering programme, where people with low incomes were invited to bring their animals or stray animals to the Refuge for neutering. David Griffiths, a veterinarian from Los Angeles who had retired to the UK, offered his services as a volunteer and this was the start of an annual event which began slowly, but soon became well known. People travelled from towns in the Burgundy region with cats and dogs they had trapped, or collected from people in rural communities who could not afford private veterinary fees.

The neutering programme was designed to train up to four veterinarians each year in neutering (especially early-age neutering) and other surgical techniques and over the years there have been veterinarians and veterinary students from Poland, Lithuania, Ukraine, USA, Belgium and France. The warm personality of David Griffiths and the free exchange of views on cultural attitudes and beliefs, helped to create an interest in global animal welfare amongst the trainees. Owners were encouraged to discuss the care of their animals with any of the veterinarians helping with the programme.

Its main aims were not just to develop the skills of the veterinarians, but to ensure that the concept of animal welfare was clearly understood by them and by the public whose animals were neutered and vaccinated. At first, local veterinarians were suspicious, thinking that a rival practice was being set up, but over the years they have gradually come to understand that such programmes assist the local veterinary profession with the promotion of animal welfare and provide a valuable service to local communities in rural areas.

Since 2000, the Humane Society of the United States/Humane Society International has helped to fund the annual neutering programme, with Neil Trent and Kelly O'Meara giving so much support and encouragement. Dogs Trust UK has provided animal handlers and other international volunteers have assisted with the programme. But each year there is still a shortfall of funds which is covered by the Refuge, such as costs for animals to be collected and returned to their owners, also food and accommodation for volunteers. Significantly, in 2006 the neutering programme was 'very successful' and no animals were turned away but the additional non-budgeted costs left us heavily in debt. It was a worrying period with grave warnings and scoldings from the charity's chartered accountant. Fortunately, a timely legacy reversed the situation.

For the past twenty years, school visits have been made by shelter volunteers on an ad hoc basis and groups of schoolchildren also visit the Refuge. The organiser of these visits is a retired schoolteacher, Josiane Cœuret, a trustee of the Refuge, who has been my 'right-hand woman' for nearly thirty years.

Rehoming animals from the Refuge is limited as prospective owners are more interested in buying a pure-bred cat or a pure-bred dog as a status symbol, than in giving an unwanted animal a home. Only 50% of the dogs in the Refuge and just 10% of the cats are adopted by families in France, but many cats brought in to us are feral and unsuitable for rehoming. Thankfully, other animals suitable for rehoming are collected from the Refuge by animal welfare organisations in neighbouring countries – Germany, Austria, Switzerland, Belgium, UK – and this makes a total of about 70% of the Refuge dogs that are rehomed each year.

Sending animals to be rehomed in other countries is not, of course, the answer to the problem of unwanted animals in France, but at least for the fortunate few, they are given another chance of life. We do euthanise animals when there are no other viable options, but unlike many animal welfare organisations around the world, to date we have faced little opposition to this policy. Occasionally a member of staff or a volunteer protests, but reluctantly ends up accepting the decision. Neutering and releasing cats is not a viable option for us, as poison is still widely used on neighbouring farmland, so I would prefer to humanely euthanise an animal rather than risk a slow painful death.

In 2004 we held our first annual animal welfare education day at the Refuge. All animal welfare societies within a 70 kilometre radius were invited, although many societies consisted of just one or two people, doing their best to help animals. The meeting was held in the top room of my house – an attic which can hold fifty people comfortably. Dr Jean-Pierre Kieffer, a veterinarian from Paris and trustee of the *Refuge de Thiernay*, spoke about farm animal welfare problems in France and Pei-Feng Su, who in 2006 founded ACTAsia, gave a presentation on her investigation into the global issue of fur farming. It was the first time that many people had ever been to a talk on animal welfare.

The combination of presenting local and international issues was a new format for the *Refuge de Thiernay* but it worked well, so was used again in future years. The dynamics of the board of trustees have changed in recent years, with new board members keen to develop educational initiatives – my long-term vision for the Refuge.

I know that the only way to change behaviour and attitudes is through the process of education, so we must find the time and money to set up some continuing education and training programmes. Life at the Refuge has been so hard over the years, with so many cruelty cases needing our help and it has always been difficult to get sufficient funds to cover our costs. I know that many other animal welfare organisations also have difficulty in raising money, so they will understand the anguish and worry that we faced.

I have tried to build up a support network through an annual magazine and regular information mail-outs and I always reply personally to everyone who gives a donation. My friends think this is unnecessary, but I believe that anyone who cares enough to help us financially deserves to be thanked personally for his or her support, as we could not continue the work of the Refuge without their donations

6

Dance, Seals and Traps

Lessons from India

Once I had set up my Refuge I still wanted to travel when my work commitments allowed and although my social life had become restricted, I was still in contact with many of my former friends. So in March 1976, six years after I opened the Refuge and some twenty years after I first met Bengt Hager and his wife Lilavati, I was invited to tour with them in India for a Festival of Dance, which had been organised by the *Conseil International de la Danse*. Knowing of my former experience working in public relations, they asked me to liaise with the media in India on behalf of the touring group, which was made up of about 100 people from Scandinavian countries.

It was a dream-come-true for me, as for most of my life I had been curious to see life in India and years before had even been invited to join a tiger hunt – needless to say, I declined – but now I would be going to India to enjoy a non-stop extravaganza of dance, a far more appealing proposition.

We visited twelve regions in India, a unique experience as we watched different regional styles of dance. Some of the traditional ones had been almost lost over time, but were now being revived and captured on film. In the state of Rajasthan I was invited to dinner at the palace of the Maharana of Udaipur, Prince Bhagwat Singh and as I walked up the steps I briefly glanced at two stuffed leopards on either side of the entrance. The maharana, who was waiting to greet us, saw me glance at them and said to me: '*I know what you are thinking, but since I've known Annabella, I've never killed another animal.*' I was slightly puzzled by his words, but as he was

1957. The beautiful ballerina Lilavati.

Credit: RdeT collection

speaking I saw a beautiful lady dressed in a sari, smiling at me. I was astonished to discover that she was Annabella Singh, whom I knew from international meetings at WSPA. I knew she was married and lived in India, but had no idea where. It was a wonderful surprise!

Annabella, who was English, was the second wife of Bhagwat Singh, the 75th Maharana of Udaipur. When Annabella was in Udaipur she was not allowed out of the palace grounds, as this was the custom for the wife of the maharana, but her husband did allow her to go discreetly to other cities in India for animal welfare reasons, wearing European dress if she wished so she would not be recognised.

The maharana respected Annabella's passion for animal welfare and set up a trust fund for her to use. It was called the Chetak Trust, named after the famous brave warhorse Chetak who carried his wounded maharana from the battlefield to safety. The fund was used to help support the Animal Birth Control (ABC) programme, set up in 1993 at Help In Suffering, Jaipur, Rajasthan.

As our dance group travelled around India, I quickly realised there were so many social issues of concern. There were so many beggars, adults and children desperately trying to survive. Some of the children seemed to be only about three or four with limbs no thicker than twigs. I learned of the caste system and how it influenced what assistance individuals could get from local benefactors. Once again I could hear my father's words '...*always remember you were born to a privileged life, so many are not so fortunate ... but should be helped whenever possible.*'

Amongst the indisputable exotic beauty of India, I was disturbed to see the heavy-laden horses and bullocks pulling carts and trailers, some animals so thin they could hardly stagger along. I went to Delhi Zoo and was appalled by the living conditions for the animals, just filthy barren prisons, no water and no shelter from the heat or the cold. When I was interviewed by the media I expressed my concerns, including my personal views that animals should not be used simply for man's pleasure – referring to the snake and mongoose fights, the zoos, and the dancing bears I had seen on the streets.

Just when I was in despair about the human suffering and the animal suffering all around me, I met Crystal Rogers, a beacon shining brightly through the darkness. Crystal was a wonderful English lady who set off from England in 1959 to start a new life in New Zealand. She stopped off in India, where she had been born, saw the miserable conditions for animals and decided to stay and do what she could to help ease their suffering. When I met her she had already set up her organisation, The Animals' Friend, with a wonderful motto, *compassion means action*. She was living a simple lifestyle in a small modest home close to Delhi, but, by 1976, through her determination and with support from friends in England, The Animals' Friend had eight staff, a dispensary for sick animals and two animal ambulances. A few years later she set up Help In Suffering in Jaipur and Compassion Unlimited Plus Action (CUPA) in Bangalore.

I started to think: could I perhaps do more for animals than just running a small animal shelter? My mind started to work overtime: perhaps a sanctuary for horses, or for farm animals? Could I find a rich donor and set up a wildlife centre? An education centre to teach children to understand and respect all animals? Could I help animal welfare in developing countries? Such ideas and many others continued to circle around in my head.

With Eurogroup for Animal Welfare

In 1980 I was asked by Mike Seymour-Rouse to help him with his exciting new project, Eurogroup for Animal Welfare. At the time Mike was the director of press and publicity for the RSPCA, UK and they had decided to set up a European coalition of animal welfarists – Eurogroup for Animal Welfare – as more and more legislation relating to animals was being decided at a European level. Mike became the first director of Eurogroup and asked me to help him identify people in France who would be able to provide scientific and technical advice on animal welfare issues to the European Commission, the Council of Ministers and the European Parliament. Of course I was delighted to help and we travelled around France to meet veterinarians, lawyers and university professors. Eventually, Mike made his selection, Dr Verron and Dr Mazetier, both excellent veterinarians in Paris.

In February 1988 I was invited by Mike to be part of a Eurogroup

1988. Prince Edward Island, Canada with a beautiful baby seal.

Credit: Mary Bloom/IFAW

delegation to visit Prince Edward Island, Canada, to see the habitat of the baby harp seals where thousands were culled each year. This visit was arranged by the International Fund for Animal Welfare (IFAW), which was lobbying the European Parliament to ban the import of seal fur pelts, in protest at the inhumane culling methods. Killing was mainly done by bludgeoning the animals to death with a 'hakapik', a long stick with a hooked blade at one end, or by shooting.

Our group flew from Boston, USA, to Prince Edward Island in two small planes, but we ran into a raging thunderstorm and had to make a detour to a neighbouring island. The next day we continued our journey to Prince Edward Island and were taken by helicopter to the ice floes, first of all viewing the whole island from the air to become oriented with the variation in landscape. Around the coastline we could see thousands of harp seals.

When we landed on the ice, the spectacle of these snow white youngsters with their large black eyes, was magical to see. Many of them seemed unconcerned that we were there, although one of our group was bitten rather badly by one of the braver young seals! The babies, which are born between November and February, have a bright

127

1988. With Trap-trap, a stray dog badly injured when caught in a leg-hold trap.

Credit: RdeT collection

1988. European Parliament, Strasbourg showing the leg-hold traps to Eileen Lemass, the MEP for Ireland.

Credit: Eurogroup for Animal Welfare

yellow colour, their fur coloured by the placental fluid, then they turn white after a few days. The pups are weaned at ten to fourteen days and start to moult in patches, leaving dense silver-grey fur with black spots and by about eighteen days, the white coat has completely gone.

Their mothers leave them on the ice and head back into the sea and go out to the estuary where the males are waiting to mate with them. A scientist who was with us was using equipment in the water to enable him to hear the sounds of the seals 'talking', the males and females calling to each other. He allowed me to listen through his headphones and also told me that each mother could hear and identify sounds made by her own baby – amazing, as there were so many. As we left the island, I felt so depressed to know that many of these beautiful young seals would soon be dead, having been slaughtered for their pelts.

In 2001, IFAW sent six veterinarians from different working backgrounds to act as licensed observers of the Canadian seal hunt. An extract from their report summary states: '*In our opinion, the 2001*

1988. At the European Parliament, Strasbourg discussing leg-hold traps with
(left to right) Lord Plumb, President of the European Parliament;
Ian Ferguson, Director of Eurogroup.

Credit: Eurogroup for Animal Welfare

*Canadian Seal Hunt is resulting in considerable and unacceptable suffering.
The adoption of a more reliable procedure for the killing of seals can
significantly reduce the present level of suffering.'*

Since my visit in 1988, more than twenty years ago, an estimated six
million seals have been clubbed or shot, primarily for their fur which
has been used by the fashion industry. Hopefully, such destructive killing
will soon be history as IFAW's press release dated 5 May 2009, states:

Historic victory for seals as EU bans trade with overwhelming majority

*The European Parliament today voted 550 to 49 in favour of a
ban on the trade of seal products within the EU ... The ban will
forbid the sale of seal products for profit within the EU with an*

130

exception for Inuit and other indigenous peoples. The International Fund for Animal Welfare (IFAW) applauded the decision as a significant victory in IFAW's 40-year campaign to end Canada's cruel commercial seal hunt.

In July 1988 Mike invited me to go to the European Parliament (EP) in Strasbourg as part of the Eurogroup delegation, to attend an exhibition on Cruelty Towards Animals, where the illegal use of leg-hold traps would be brought to the attention of the Members of the European Parliament (MEPs). The traps were a scourge in rural France at the time and so many animals such as foxes, dogs and cats were regularly caught in these terrible traps, the heavy steel jaws trapping and crushing a limb, making it impossible for the animal to escape. Often a limb would be ripped off, or an animal would gnaw its own leg until it could struggle free, or the animal would die in the trap in agony. Sometimes a domestic pet would manage to get home, dragging the trap, still attached to the crushed limb. In such situations the animals either died of shock or injury, or at best, the limb would need to be amputated. In preparation for the meeting at the EP, I enlisted the help of my friends to search junk shops and street markets to buy any leg-hold traps they could find and then I prepared for my visit to Strasbourg.

The day arrived and I walked into the EP with six heavy traps around my neck. The effect was exactly what I had hoped for, causing great attention with numerous questions asked by the MEPs. I was able to explain just how cruel these traps were and how domestic pets could easily get caught. At the time there were twelve member countries of Eurogroup and half of these were still using these traps. Barbara Castle, an MEP and former UK Minister of Transport, showed great interest in the traps I had brought into the Parliament, as did some other MEPs, but sadly none of the French delegation seemed concerned.

The European Parliament EP News, (UK edition) 4–8 July 1988 showed a photograph of Barbara Castle and me holding a leg-hold trap, with the caption:

'Outlaw these death traps ... Two women with a single purpose ... Barbara Castle and Princess Elisabeth de Croÿ are pushing the campaign to have leghold traps outlawed... '

The report continues:

Animal traps ban proposed

An exhibition illustrating cruelty to animals staged on the initiative of Barbara Castle (Greater Manchester West. Soc.) with the support of the all-party intergroup on animal welfare, was held in the Parliament's building in Strasbourg from July 5–8. Representatives from animal welfare groups throughout the Community were present, including Catherine, Princess Aga Khan, who has campaigned against the fur trade and Princess Elisabeth de Croÿ of the French Animal Protection Council.

The exhibition featured examples of cruelty to animals that still take place either through blood sports, intensive farming or laboratory testing.

One issue of particular concern to members of the group, is the continued use of leghold traps by fur hunters.

In 1995, seven years later, the EU banned the use of leg-hold traps in Europe and also banned the importation of pelts from animals killed in such traps.

Practically all my travels and accommodation in various countries have been either sponsored, or through the generosity of friends. When my mother died in 1977 at the age of eighty-eight, there was little cash value in her estate and what she had was divided among her eight children, so each of us received just a very small legacy. As mentioned in an earlier chapter, my grandfather was disinherited by his father for marrying my English grandmother and therefore forfeited considerable wealth and family assets. The main part of my mother's estate was Château d'Azy, the contents and the land. My unmarried sister Catherine continued to live at the château but the ongoing maintenance costs for a castle of such huge proportions were formidable.

I realised right from the early days at the *Refuge de Thiernay* that although I had little money, I did have something almost as useful – my privileged background and titles! This could help me with humanitarian and animal welfare activities; it was my unique selling point, or USP, in marketing terminology. I didn't have any money to give away or any special skills to offer, but I did have several titles which could be used to open doors. I have also been able to use my USP to assist others, by, for example, writing letters on their behalf to secure meetings with high-profile people, by giving personal recommendations to speed up bureaucratic procedures, or to get media coverage, simply on the strength of using my name. I do not use my titles in my everyday life for vanity or personal benefit and as I have no children, the titles will die with me, but during my lifetime, for the potential benefit of humans and animals, I will continue to exploit my USP.

However there have been occasions when my titles have gone against me, as it is assumed that I am wealthy so my charity doesn't need donations or financial support although once people visit my home, this view is immediately reversed!

2003: Campaigning with Naturewatch UK in Kiev.

7

Missions in Eastern Europe

Aid for Poland

In the 1980s, a supporter from the Aix-en-Provence region adopted a dog from my Refuge. He was the Mayor of Prémery at the time and had a lovely daughter who worked in human welfare. She was organising a visit to Poland to take medicines and supplies for the hospitals and monasteries and invited me to go with her. Having been to Hungary in 1957, I had followed the political situation in Eastern Europe over the years from limited media information and I was curious to know more about the philosophy of communist rule and indeed curious to see how it could realistically work in practice. I eagerly accepted the offer and in November 1986 we set off in a lorry, full of supplies, for the journey across land to Poland.

Countries in Central and Eastern Europe were still in the grip of the Soviet Union in 1986, but there was growing unrest and demonstrations had started as discontented citizens started to rebel against Russian domination. The cold war had succeeded in isolating these countries from the rest of the world and the social conditions of the populations were now dire. The Soviet Union was on the verge of bankruptcy and I knew that people had little money as their wages were often unpaid; shops had few goods to sell, with medication, equipment and other necessities for hospitals in drastically short supply.

In 1986 I found Poland to be as I had imagined, drab and depressing, grey in colour and atmosphere compared to countries in Western Europe; devoid of colourful advertising posters or attractive shop window displays. In general the faces of people in the streets appeared blank or wary; there seemed to be little cheer and few smiles. But staff at the hospitals and clinics where we took the donated medications and supplies were so happy to receive us and they appreciated the support from the donors in France. These dedicated hospital staff really touched my heart as they devotedly carried out their work in crumbling buildings, doing the best they could with broken and outdated equipment.

We took supplies to several hospitals in Warsaw, Kraków and Wroclaw and to monasteries of the Capuchin and Benedictine monks, but at each place so much more than we had to give, was desperately needed, such as clothes, books, basic household equipment, food and machinery.

On the streets we saw thin, disease-ridden dogs and cats, also malnourished working horses pulling carts, but when we spoke to the authorities and veterinarians about these issues, although fully aware of the problems, they were powerless to act as they had few resources. I decided that on my return to France I must do something to help both humans and animals in Poland and would try to find sponsors to donate goods and medication.

1989. Arriving at a monastery in Poland with donated supplies from France.

Credit: Jenny Remfry

1989. Jenny Remfry (right) with the Manager of the Wrocław branch of TOZ.

Credit: Jenny Remfry

Once home in France, I contacted the media and explained the situation in Poland and what I wanted to do. Immediately there was a positive response from the public and amongst others, a wealthy Polish lady living in the south of France, gave a very large donation. The pharmacy in Nevers, run by the Vaslin family was most generous and donated large quantities of drugs and supplies. Other people were also generous and gave clothes and household supplies such as tea, coffee and soap.

Such support was wonderful and two years after my first visit we were able to hire a large lorry and fill it with 500 kilo of medical supplies: needles, syringes, intravenous drips, bandages, antibiotics, ointments, vitamins, calcium, medication for heart conditions and other health problems, clothes, books, toys, also veterinary supplies for sterilising dogs and cats – with specific medications for the treatment of skin problems and other ailments.

I asked Dr Jenny Remfry, a UK veterinarian who was on the staff of WSPA's office in London, to come to Poland with me, as I wanted to maximise the effect of the visit. I knew that Jenny was experienced in negotiating with government officials and veterinarians, so she was the ideal person to accompany me. She was also practical and jolly.

We set off in April 1989 and drove from Nevers to Strasbourg where we stopped off at the European Parliament as they were holding meetings that included debates on bullfighting and the illegal use of leg-hold traps; topics of great interest to me. We stayed in Strasbourg overnight with Dr and Mme Wernert, supporters of my Refuge and then continued on our way, eventually arriving at the monastery in Wroclaw where we stayed overnight as guests of the Capuchin monks. We had taken supplies for them, which included much-needed oil, soap and medicines.

In Warsaw we made contact with *Towarzystwo Opieki nad Zwierzętami w Polsce* (TOZ), the National Society for the Protection of Animals and learned of the realities facing them; the lack of money and resources and so many other animal welfare issues that needed to be tackled. But as the country was practically in ruins, it was a formidable task.

We visited several shelters in different areas of Poland; many were just hovels and it defies any attempt to describe accurately just how inadequate they were for the needs of the dogs and cats. But how can one be judgemental and righteous in a country where people have lived under persecution and repression for so many years? I am ashamed to admit that on some occasions I was probably far too harsh and outspoken and was indeed openly critical of the appalling facilities.

We visited Torun, a beautiful medieval town in the north of Poland (which became a listed UNESCO World Heritage Site in 1997) and made contact with the municipality. Surprisingly, this was the first step of a new beginning. Soon after our visit, I was asked to help and advise on the construction of a new animal shelter in Torun. I immediately contacted Graham Fuller at WGAS and he asked his shelter consultant, Bill Hames to visit Torun. Bill's visit to advise on plans for the new shelter was financed by the Polish lady in France who had already donated a substantial amount and she continued to sponsor additional visits, for Bill to monitor the progress of the shelter. The Polish manager of the Torun shelter visited my Refuge in France to see how a simple basic shelter could be effective and together we visited WGAS in the UK for a meeting with Graham and Bill. When the Torun shelter was completed in the mid-1990s, it became a flagship centre for animal welfare in Poland.

I returned to Poland in 1993 as a WSPA Advisory Director with Janice Cox, WSPA director for Central and Eastern Europe, to visit veterinarians, government officials and animal welfare groups. By this time the cold war was over and charities from Western Europe were able to provide more humanitarian aid for Eastern European countries. Janice had already made contact with many pioneering animal welfarists in several ex-Soviet countries and was working on training programmes to help them understand the basic concepts of animal welfare and importantly, how to impart this information to others. Janice was the perfect person to do this pioneering work as she had a calm non-judgemental approach, always smiling, with kind words for those who were trying to do their best. Even when the situation was somewhat grim, she continued to support and encourage, as opposed to being openly critical. I wish I had some of her qualities, but alas, there are still many occasions when I am too impatient and judgemental.

On this visit to Poland we were accompanied by Derek Evans, a WSPA consultant veterinarian and Steve Cox, Janice's husband. I felt very happy and safe to have Steve travelling with us, for besides being great fun he was a security consultant specialising in personal protection worldwide. Both Derek and Steve were most security-conscious and kept reminding Janice and me to keep tight hold of our bags and wallets.

We were travelling in Poland by train and one day as the train approached the platform and slowed to a halt, we got on. There were many other people scrambling to do the same, but as I tried to move into an empty space, a man stood blocking my way as others bundled into us. I pushed my way into the space and Janice, Derek and Steve followed. Steve suddenly saw his comb on the floor of the carriage which alerted his suspicions. Immediately he reached into his pocket for his wallet – it was no longer there. Derek realising what had happened, checked his pockets, alas, his wallet had also disappeared. The two men were so annoyed and frustrated when they realised that the scramble and jostling from others getting on to the train, were all part of the thieves' planned mugging. Thankfully, Janice and I still had our bags and wallets. What a disaster, but how Janice and I laughed at the expense of our unfortunate security-conscious companions!

In less than twenty years, Poland has now changed from a communist state in chaos, to a progressive democracy which has given rise to a new generation of motivated and optimistic young people. Of course there are still social problems to overcome, including a legacy of corruption and persecution, but life in Poland, as in other former Soviet countries, has become one of hope instead of despair.

I went to Poland nine times between 1986 and 1996, each time taking aid for people and animals, donated by caring people in France. I met many strong, determined people in Poland with pioneering spirit, such as Dr Pawel Novak, a veterinarian from Wroclaw and Ewa Gebert from Gdansk, who still continues to battle through red tape and campaigns on companion animal and farm animal welfare issues through her organisation (OTOZ); the Polish Society for the Protection of Animals, which she established in 2000.

I recall that the first conference on stray animal control in Poland was organised by Ewa in the early 1990s and I was an invited guest. One of the presentations was given by a veterinarian on the controversial issue of euthanasia, as an option for diseased and aggressive dogs. Euthanasia was a taboo subject for many attending and one lady wept copious tears, clearly distressed. Although none of the local people had any viable solutions for managing the overpopulation of dogs in Poland, few at the conference could bear to hear about euthanasia. One lady described to me after the conference how any discussion on euthanasia in shelters brought back memories of the gas chambers in the concentration camps of Poland, where her family members were killed. She too had been in a concentration camp as a small child, but was liberated at the end of the war and liberation (meaning a new home in this context) was her dream for all of the shelter animals, regardless of their health or temperament status. How can any of us who have never had to endure such terrible experiences, possibly understand such comparisons? We can't.

On a lighter note, that evening I unexpectedly received a proposal of marriage from our amusing consultant veterinarian, Ray Butcher, who had started to relax with a tipple or two, or three, after the demanding conference, when he suddenly dropped to one knee in a crowded restaurant and asked me to marry him. Of course I was flattered as he was more than thirty years younger than me, but I declined the proposition as I thought that his sweet wife Moira may not have been too keen on the idea!

Over the years my involvement with Poland and especially the construction of the Torun shelter, was incredibly frustrating at times, as the bureaucratic procedures created endless delays. However as time went by I met some remarkable people in Eastern European countries and admired the tenacious efforts of those who emerged from the communist era with determination and vision. This in turn motivated me to keep going, knowing that metaphorically there are those who have much higher mountains to climb than we have in France, yet who will not give up while there is so much to do.

Such a person is Marcela Lund, a successful businesswoman and a strong-minded lady who has become a dear friend. Marcela was a founding member of *Nadace Na Ochranu Zvířat* (the Animal Protection Trust) in 1994 in the Czech Republic and since the organisation began she has tirelessly led, promoted and supported Nadace, with their campaigns and progressive educational initiatives. Although maintaining her business commitments as well as overseeing the Animal Protection Trust, Marcela has still found time to support and encourage the work of groups in other countries, especially Slovakia, as well as the work of groups in other parts of the world. She even found ways to support me when I had some difficulties at my Refuge a few years ago. She is indeed a true friend for animal welfare.

Children and Animals: Ukraine

In 1996 when international animal welfare organisations found the political and economic complexities of Ukraine too difficult to penetrate, Naturewatch UK started to collaborate with Tamara Tarnawska and the Kiev Society for the Protection of Animals – SOS (SPA-SOS) – by offering support for the SPA-SOS animal shelter that was in the process of being converted from a former budka. A budka is a place where dogs and cats are taken and killed for their fur, which is then sold and used in the making of clothes and accessories, with many of the skins sent to China for processing. Horrific reports of animals being cruelly killed and some even skinned while still alive had been rife for many years, with covert filming available to confirm the reports.

141

SOS-SPA Kiev Press Conference.
Left to right: Christian Janatsch, President of Tierhilfswerk; me; Tamara Tarnawska,
President of SPA-SOS; Bohdan Nahajlo; Caroline Barker and John Ruane, Naturewatch.

Credit: Naturewatch

For more than fifteen years, Tamara Tarnawska, a formidable lady, has bravely lobbied the authorities initially to close the budka in Kiev and to introduce legislation to protect all animals. Her efforts are supported by John Ruane and Naturewatch, and with their help Tamara has now achieved both these missions and has transformed the budka, a place of killing, into an animal shelter – a place of caring. Also in April 2006, the Animal Protection Bill became law, a great triumph, but now the legislation has to be enforced, so pressure on the government still has to be maintained.

In 1997, as an Advisory Director of WSPA, I went to Kiev for the official opening of the SPA-SOS shelter at Pyrohovo and gave a media conference in support of Tamara and her animal welfare initiatives. Christian Janatsch from *Tierhilfswerk Austria* was also in Kiev as he and his team have been a wonderful support to SPA-SOS almost from the beginning of the organisation, providing veterinary equipment, manpower, finance and expertise.

Unlike Poland, Ukraine has struggled to establish itself as a true democratic country and continues to be politically and economically unstable. This has had a marked effect on the progress of animal welfare, as those in government positions with the power to make changes, are often 'here today and gone tomorrow', so the lack of continuity is a frustrating reality of life in Ukraine.

I have been there five times in the past twelve years, on four occasions as an ambassador for Naturewatch, and am full of admiration for Tamara and her colleagues as they have never been deterred from their mission – even when Tamara was held in prison on trumped-up charges.

On my first visit to Ukraine in 1997 I could see depression and signs of poverty all around me; vehicles were old; many people were wearing threadbare clothes and there was practically no food to buy in the shops, so it was not surprising that the plight of animals was a low priority for most people. There was no legislation to protect animals, so the situation at the budkas was not an issue for government concern, likewise Kiev zoo, a place where hundreds of animals were dying each year through disease and malnutrition.

I knew before going to Ukraine that there were many hospitals

Arriving in Ukraine with donated toys and clothes.

Credit: RdeT collection

and orphanages in desperate need of financial help and supplies, so I had carried as many clothes, toys and soap as I could and battled my way through the rigours of the customs authorities at the airport. I asked Tamara if she could arrange for me to go to a children's hospital so she organised our travel to the Chernihiv Region Children's Hospital, about 130 kilometres north of Kiev.

On the way we were stopped by the police who said we were breaking the speed limit – we were not. I was later told that it was an excuse for the police to stop cars and demand an on-the-spot penalty, which allegedly goes no further than the policeman's pocket. Our driver said to the policeman that he was not aware that he was breaking the speed limit and was driving carefully as he was taking a European princess to visit the hospital. I smiled and spoke very politely to the police officers and we were allowed to continue our journey without paying a fine.

The hospital was located in an area badly affected by the Chernobyl nuclear power plant disaster in 1986, when an accident caused a massive release of radioactivity into the environment, contaminating large areas. The Chernobyl accident is ranked by the International Nuclear Event Scale as Level 7, the only such disaster ever to reach this level, making it the worst nuclear power plant disaster in history, with countries throughout Europe affected by the radioactive contamination.

There were about five hundred children at the hospital with the majority suffering from cancer as a result of the devastating nuclear eruption and each year more than 12,000 were treated and hospitalised, all suffering from cancer or other serious illnesses.

I was taken around the hospital and was so moved by the sight of so many ill children. I was introduced to a very sick child who loved cats and fortunately I had a lovely soft black and white cuddly toy cat with me, so I was able to give it to her. She put it on her pillow and I was later told that it stayed with her on the pillow until she died, just two weeks later.

The facilities were so much better than I expected and the hospital appeared to be efficiently managed, with the wards clean and tidy and the nurses smartly dressed in uniform, attending to the children's needs. I understand that many hospitals in Ukraine are not so well maintained and that Chernihiv is an exception, so I left the hospital determined to help any of the hospitals and mentally prepared for my next visit to Ukraine.

I met Monsieur Roland Pallade, a Frenchman managing the *Crédit Agricole Bank* in Kiev and he told me about other needy centres – the orphanages and the destitute old people's homes – and arranged for me to meet Sister Marie Louis from the Order of St Joseph. She cares for the poorest of the poor elderly people in a hospital located on the outskirts of Kiev and often works in tandem with Mother Teresa's Sisters.

I knew that I could help with clothes and other essentials for these charities but needed to be able to take excess baggage and get through customs without having the goods confiscated; at the time this was difficult in Ukraine.

On my return from Kiev to Paris, I sent the following letter to the president of Air Ukraine International:

Dear Mr Miroshnikov
I am writing to you with regards to my forthcoming visit to the Ukraine for which I wish to bring excess baggage and require some assistance. Having visited the Chernihiv Hospital specialising in the care of children with cancer on a previous occasion, I was so moved by the level of care and dedication of the staff and volunteers and I vowed I would try to do a little to help. The hospital was impeccable and the level of care given is something seldom seen in life. This has left a deep impression on me and driven me to do something to help. With the numbers of children at the hospital, I felt that some assistance could be given in the way of donation of clothes, toys, medicines, etc.

The excess baggage I would like to bring is made up of donations I have collected as gifts for the children and I would be most grateful for your assistance to give me free excess baggage. The gifts are to be given to the children at Chernihiv Hospital and also the Internat Velyki Mezhyitchi Orphanage…

Mr Miroshnikov agreed to a most generous allowance of free excess baggage, so on my next visit to the hospital I again carried as much as I could with me but I still had to fight to get the donated goods through customs.

145

In total I made just two visits to the children's hospital and one visit to the orphanage, which was located 300 kilometres west of Kiev in an old eighteenth-century palace. An accident in France, followed by an operation in 2006, curtailed any further visits which was most unfortunate as I particularly wanted to revisit the orphanage where there were 130 children aged between seven and seventeen, all with slight mental disabilities. Their chances of being adopted were indeed slim, so any attention from regular visitors would give them something to look forward to. Sadly, visitors were few and far between.

Complications developed after my operation and now with permanent disability, my travels have become limited in recent years and unfortunately, despite much effort from several individuals who tried to break through the layers of bureaucracy, I was unable to send the medical supplies generously donated by pharmacies and hospitals in France.

However Monsieur Pallade has kindly taken donated goods to Ukraine for me and I am delighted to learn of support for some of the children's hospitals and orphanages in Ukraine, provided by the Maria Sharapover Foundation and the United Nations Development Programme.

Monsieur Pallade is now back in Paris as his former bank in Kiev became the Calyon Bank. But before leaving he arranged for Anatoliy Pavlovskiy, head of general services at the bank, to receive any donations of clothes, toys etc. and distribute them where there is the most need. At the time of writing, my attic is holding numerous boxes awaiting collection for Ukraine.

In 2005 I was presented with the Ukraine Ministry of Culture's Award by Mr Prystavskyi, Deputy Minister of Culture, in recognition of my contribution to the management of stray animals. Although I was honoured, I felt there were others far more deserving than me, as I could walk away from the situation and return to my country where life is less restrictive. With all the long-term effects from years of communist rule in Ukraine and the ongoing consequences of the worst nuclear power plant disaster in history, it is indeed a tribute to humanity that many people in Ukraine are doing what they can to help people and animals in need.

8

International Ambassador

Dancing Bears in Turkey

I was invited by WSPA to go to Turkey in my capacity as a WSPA Advisory Director to officially open the outside enclosure for rescued dancing bears at the new wildlife centre. I was so thrilled to be asked to do this as I knew Victor Watkins and had followed his Libearty Campaign since it began. Also my staff at the Refuge had raised funds to support the campaign.

I had seen dancing bears on the streets of Turkey and it broke my heart to see such magnificent creatures reduced to pathetic 'robots', as their owners dragged them along, pulling the ropes and chains to make them perform when a tourist showed interest. Although WSPA was building a semi-wild sanctuary in the forest, after the bears were rescued they first had to be given veterinary treatment. They would then need to be observed and assessed in a two-acre enclosure over a period of time, before going to the semi-wild sanctuary.

WSPA's Libearty Campaign, the brainchild of Victor Watkins, WSPA's Director of Wildlife, was introduced in 1991 to protect the dwindling wild populations of bears. The campaign quickly captured the attention and interest of the general public as reports on dancing bears in Greece and Turkey hit the media. Bears were also hunted in Turkey for trophies and skins and often shot by villagers when they strayed from the forests, so the survival of bears in Turkey was under serious threat. In the early 1990s it was estimated that there were about twenty dancing bears in Greece and up to one hundred in Turkey.

Traditionally, dancing bears were kept by gypsy families in many

147

1988. Dancing bear with gypsy owner waiting for tourists in Istanbul, Turkey.

Credit: Jeremy Leney

countries for economic reasons, in Greece, Turkey, India, Bulgaria and Romania. When the head of a gypsy family was nearing the end of his life, he asked other family members to promise that they would always have a dancing bear, so they could earn money and provide for the family. Thankfully, owning a dancing bear is a tradition that has been declining over the last century, but still exists, mainly in India.

The bears are taken from the wild as cubs, their mothers often shot while trying to protect them. The young bears are then raised with gypsy families and usually fed on a poor diet, mainly bread, so as they grow they are likely to develop tooth decay and other more serious medical problems.

To control the growing bear, his nose or lip is pierced, then a large metal ring inserted (sometimes more than one ring) without giving the animal any anaesthetics or pain relief. A rope is attached to the ring to enable the handler to 'manage' the bear.

While still a young cub, the bear is taught to 'dance' on a hot metal plate and when the gypsy handler bangs on a tambourine or a similar instrument, the poor bear lifts his feet in agony as the burning metal scalds his paws: this is called dancing! The bear quickly learns to lift up his feet whenever he hears the sound of a tambourine and is taken by his owner to popular areas of the town to beg for money. Tourists seeing this spectacle for the first time are often excited and give money in exchange for watching the bear 'dance' – not realising the torture and lifetime of misery endured by the animal.

In 1992 the Turkish Ministry of Tourism agreed to work with WSPA's Libearty team on a plan to protect wild bears roaming the forests of Turkey and to stop the appalling spectacle of dancing bears. It was agreed to build a wildlife and rescue centre and rescue all of the dancing bears. As there were too many bears to rescue at the same time, it was decided that the bears performing on the streets of Istanbul would be the first to be rescued.

In 1993 the Wildlife and Rescue Centre was built at Uladag University in Bursa, about 200 kilometres from Istanbul, where an empty warehouse was converted into a wildlife veterinary centre. The rescue of Turkey's dancing bears began.

I proudly opened the WSPA bear enclosure on 11 November 1994.

1994. Opening of the first bear enclosure at the Wildlife and Rescue Centre,
University of Uladag, Turkey. This young bear arrived and was named 'Elisabeth'.

Credit: JLL/WSPA

There were thousands of people at the opening, including the Governor
of Bursa and the Rector of Uladag University and there was also extensive
media coverage. Birgul Rhona from the Turkish animal welfare society
Turkiye Hayvanlari Koruma Dernegi (THKD) was there, beaming so
happily. She had worked tirelessly with Victor and his team for several
years, investigating sightings of dancing bears; liaising with the Turkish
authorities and lobbying government officials to enforce the law, as the
practice of dancing bears was actually illegal in Turkey.

Seven of the rescued adult bears were released into the enclosure
that day and the others were going to be gradually released in stages.
In the enclosure there were fruit bushes, pine trees and soft earth so
the bears could forage for insects and fruit. There was a swimming
pool which overflowed so there was lots of mud for them to roll in
and concrete dens filled with straw. These bears had been on chains
most of their lives, never freely interacting with other bears, never
being able to swim or forage for food.

It was simply wonderful and so moving to see them take their first steps to freedom; I am so proud to have been part of that day. An unexpected event was the arrival of a young female cub brought all the way from east Anatolia – sadly her mother had been shot by hunters. As she arrived on the day I opened the bear enclosure she was named Elisabeth after me and I was overcome with emotion!

Sadly, several of the rescued dancing bears were either blind or partly blind, the results of a poor diet, and many had severe dental problems arising from broken teeth, mouth infections and abscesses, but they were given the best possible veterinary treatment by WSPA through their consultant veterinarian, Dr Dorrestein, Director of the Utrecht University Wildlife Department. But most of all, they were free.

Pet Respect Campaign: Taiwan

I was so excited to get a phone call from Joy Leney one morning asking if I would go to Taiwan as an ambassador on behalf of WSPA. At the time I was a WSPA Advisory Director and Joy was WSPA Director for Asia, working on the stray animal problem in Taiwan with Wu Hung and Pei-Feng Su, co-founders of the organisation Life Conservationist Association (LCA) of Taiwan. They were arranging a 'Pet Respect' conference in Taipei to introduce humane methods of stray dog management.

At the time the methods used in Taiwan for dealing with stray and unwanted dogs and cats were horrific, such as clubbing to death, drowning, burning alive, starvation, electrocution – so inhumane – but as there was little, if any, understanding of animals as sentient beings, it was cruelty through ignorance and indifference, rather than deliberate cruelty. Wu Hung and his volunteers had investigated several of the government dog pounds and documented the most appalling evidence of abuse and mistreatment. As a result of their meetings with government officials, the Pet Respect conference was sponsored by Taiwan's Council of Agriculture and the Environmental Protection Agency, with attendance from many government departments.

The day arrived in February 1995 for us to set off with a small team: UK animal wardens Mandy Thompson and Kevin Cope and a wonderful veterinarian who has become a dear friend, John Gripper,

1995. The government dog pound at Pan Chiao, Taiwan.

Credit: LCA

1995. Preparing for the WSPA Pet Respect Conference in Taiwan. Left to right: Mandy Thompson; Joy Leney; Taipei official; me; Kevin Cope.

Credit: LCA

152

1995.Wu Hung demonstrating a dog catching wire on me.

Credit: LCA

1995. Meeting at Taiwan Council of Agriculture to discuss the stray animal problem.
Left to right: Mr Lin Hsiang-nung (Deputy Minister/Chairman); me; Joy Leney (WSPA).

Credit: LCA

153

who is also an Advisory Director of WSPA. (John and his lovely wife Annie have their own charity, Sebakwe Black Rhino Trust, which they set up in 1988 to protect these magnificent endangered animals.)

We arrived at Taipei airport and were warmly welcomed by Wu Hung and Pei-Feng. I was enchanted with the serene way in which the Buddhist monk Wu Hung seemed to glide through the crowds at the airport, with people standing back in respect as he passed through. I was to learn a lot more about this very special person, who will have my greatest respect to my dying day.

The following day we were taken to see the municipal dog catchers at work. As we drove around the streets we saw them trying to catch the numerous stray dogs – not with humane equipment, but with thin wires which they expertly looped over the dog's head and pulled immediately to tighten the wire around the dog's throat. Of course the terrified dogs screamed in pain, but their cries were ignored as they were dangled above the ground by their necks and thrown into the back of the waiting truck.

1999. WSPA exhibition stand at Crufts Dog Show. Left to right: Trevor Wheeler; Joy Leney; Claire Palmer; Pei-Feng Su; me.

Credit: David Paton

We followed the truck to the government dog pound – and what a shock! Several hundred dogs were crammed into small cages, some of them were dead, some dying, one was even giving birth. I witnessed dogs being dragged out of the cages and taken to the gas chamber. It was a terrible experience for me, but oh so much worse for the poor dogs.

In contrast, the three-day conference was a much happier experience. Pei-Feng and her volunteers had arranged everything to perfection. Senior officials from all relevant government departments attended and as I opened the conference I urged the government to introduce legislation for the humane treatment of all animals. I still recall the panic and fear in the eyes of the dogs at the dog pound and can still hear their screams as they were being caught with those dreadful thin pieces of wire: a haunting experience.

Taiwan became a very special place for me. I loved the beautiful temples and museums, the delightful people and the lasting friendship with Wu Hung and Pei-Feng. Several Taiwanese students and animal welfare volunteers have been to stay at my home in Thiernay for work experience; I also adopted six stray dogs from Taiwan, one being 'the love of my life', who I called Panchiao, the name of the place from where he was rescued.

The Animal Protection Law was passed in Taiwan in 1995, thanks to lobbying by animal activists in Taiwan and international pressure.

Mexican Dog

Over the years I have felt instantly drawn to certain animals when visiting other countries, so have succumbed to bringing them back to France. I have brought about ten dogs back home in total during a thirty-year period to either rehome, or to become my personal dogs. It seems a pointless thing to do as there are many dogs needing homes in France, but sometimes even the most rational individuals at times do something unpredictable!

In 1994 I almost brought an unwanted dog back to France from Mexico, but thankfully a good home was found in the USA. I was in New York for the American Society for the Prevention of Cruelty

1994. Whilst in New York, Amelia arranged for me to visit LEMSIP:
Laboratory for Experimental Medicine and Surgery in Primates,
New York University Research Facility, USA.

Credit: Amelia Tarzi

to Animals (ASPCA) Henry Bergh Award Ceremony, as I was a
recipient that year, so took the opportunity to travel on to Mexico
with my friend Amelia for a sightseeing holiday. We used a basic
hotel in Guadalajara as our base and enjoyed ourselves visiting temples
and ancient sites.

Two days before we were due to leave Mexico, we were at Lake
Chapala when we suddenly saw a young boy aged about eight, pulling
a puppy by its tail up a flight of steps. The poor puppy was yelping
in fright and pain, as its head bumped on every step. We rushed up
to him and Amelia, who could speak fluent Spanish, told him to
stop what he was doing immediately and where was his mother? He
pointed to a door and his mother appeared. At first, she said it was
their dog and then she said it wasn't and would we please take it
away? It obviously was their dog, but now they didn't want it, so
what could we do?

The puppy was only about ten weeks old, scrawny and full of fleas,
so we decided to take it back with us to the hotel and then decide what

to do next. One problem was that no animals were allowed in the hotel, so we had a brainwave: we would buy some ponchos and Amelia would pretend to be pregnant holding the dog underneath the poncho against her tummy. We found a shop that sold large heavy ponchos, not ideal, as the weather was so hot, but the store owner had no idea we wanted to wear them straightaway, and thought we were taking them home as gifts. On the way back to the hotel we bought some deworming medicine for the puppy, but it was actually for pigs, not puppies, so we had to work out a smaller dose.

When we got to the hotel we had to climb over a fence and go through the back entrance, to avoid meeting any hotel staff as they had already seen Amelia and knew that she was not pregnant. Once in our room, we dewormed the puppy. Oh dear, the medication worked very well and within a few hours there were worms all over the floor of our room, which we cleaned up as best we could.

We were leaving Mexico the following morning and had to fly to Mexico City first, then on to New York. If only we could take the puppy with us, but there was no time to get the necessary export papers ... or so we thought. What should we do with her? We decided to go to a top class hotel for our last day in Mexico, where there were likely to be people staying with dogs and perhaps someone would give our little dog a home, or we could pay someone to keep her until we could make other arrangements.

We donned our ponchos with the little dog well hidden under Amelia's poncho and found a taxi. Amelia did a brilliant impersonation of a pregnant woman, by carefully waddling along the street, then cautiously getting into the taxi with me acting the part of the caring grandmother-to-be. On the way to the hotel I suddenly saw a sign for a veterinary clinic and yelled at the bemused taxi driver to stop.

We got out of the cab and went into the veterinary clinic where I told the veterinarian that we had owned the dog for a few weeks and wanted an export health certificate. He examined it and sprayed it for fleas, gave it an injection and started to fill out the forms. '*What is her name?*' the veterinarian asked. Amelia's face suddenly looked blank and I quickly said: '*It's Betsy.*' I'm not sure that the veterinarian believed anything we told him, but he went along with us and we left his clinic with the health certificate and a small travelling box for the dog, in readiness for the flight to Mexico City. Another problem was that animals were not allowed on the flight, so at the airport Amelia again acted out her role as an expectant mother-to-be and we just walked nonchalantly through security, unhindered, with the dog and its carrying box hidden under Amelia's poncho. Fortunately the little dog who seemed to know what to do was quiet on the plane and on arrival at New York, we again walked through security and customs without any searches or questioning.

The next hurdle was the journey by train from New York to Washington. The animals were not allowed to travel with their owners on the train, but by now the puppy was used to being submerged under a heavy poncho. We sat opposite a man who was on his own and he kept looking at us and smiling. Was he flirting with us? If so, I'm not sure why, as Amelia was heavily pregnant and I was seventy-three. We ignored him and eventually he lost interest in us. Suddenly the puppy gave a couple of muffled barks; Amelia and I were alarmed, but just laughed and pretended to cough. The man looked up and said: '*I can also bark, girls,*' and he started imitating the barking noise that he thought we had made. What a bizarre journey!

We stayed with Anne Cottrell-Free, a journalist friend in Washington and had dinner with Christine Stevens, founder of the Animal Welfare Institute, who found the story so funny. It has a happy ending as Anne's daughter Elissa who worked at CNN found the puppy a home with one of her colleagues who was relocating to Florida.

I hasten to add that I do not advocate smuggling dogs across borders and now fifteen years later with much tighter controls on security, it would probably be impossible to do so without detection, so I won't be doing it again.

Crete Shelter: Greece

The Greek Animal Welfare Fund (GAWF) shelter was located in the mountains of Athlada on the Greek island of Crete. It housed about 120 animals and the shelter was built with donations from supporters. The dogs were housed in large enclosures in groups of six to eight.

1996. David Barnes and volunteers receiving the dogs from the Crete Athlada Shelter at the airport in Nevers.

Credit: GAWF/RdeT

However, despite the best intentions of the staff and repeated attempts to manage the shelter humanely, it was impossible. Greek law did not allow anyone to live at the site which meant that the animals were unsupervised after 4 p.m. so if a fight developed between any of the dogs, injuries were not discovered and treated until the following morning. Indeed, on occasions, dogs attacked by their canine companions died overnight.

The shelter was almost inaccessible to the public as it was way off the main road. Also taxi drivers were reluctant to venture on to the stony track leading to the shelter as their vehicles would almost certainly be damaged by stones and rubble flying up from under the wheels, so visitors seldom went to the shelter to adopt animals.

Some of the animals had been at the shelter for several years, but sadly their ultimate fate was likely to be determined by disease or injury. In 1996, GAWF's Council of Management decided to close the Athlada shelter on the condition that all animals suitable for adoption would be found new homes. This was an anxious time as there were 120 animals – donkeys, cats, and dogs – resident there.

David Barnes, a former RSPCA inspector and shelter manager, was hired to arrange and coordinate the project, including relocation of the animals. Dr Roger Mugford, the high-profile UK animal psychologist (also consultant for the Queen's dogs), travelled to Crete to assess each animal's suitability for rehoming and made psychological profiles of all the animals. Manolis Alexakis, GAWF's representative in Crete, made all the necessary arrangements with the Greek authorities for the export of the animals.

The donkeys were rehomed in Cyprus into the care of Patrick and Mary Skinner who ran the excellent rescue centre 'Friends of the Cyprus Donkey' at Vouni, near Limassol. The cats stayed in Crete with Vagelis and Anna Grammatikaki at Carteros Farm Riding Centre, where they could stroll around the farm or hide in the numerous barns doing what cats do best. But where could sixty dogs be rehomed? The dogs would almost certainly be adopted if sent to the UK, but the cost of transporting sixty dogs to the UK plus costs for six months' quarantine, made this an unfeasible option.

I was a patron of GAWF and immediately said that some of the dogs could come to the *Refuge de Thiernay* and I would do my best to find homes for them through my contacts in European countries such as Holland and Germany, where the quarantine requirements were more flexible, although just as effective. David liaised with me to make sure that each animal had the correct legal paperwork required by the French veterinary services and all health issues were covered before the dogs left Greece.

After several weeks of preparation and repeated veterinary checks, the dogs were ready to leave Crete by air, the Ukrainian plane having been chartered at a discounted rate. The canine cargo was loaded and the journey began. The first stop was Bratislava in Slovakia to refuel, then back in the air and on to France.

I arranged for the plane to land at a small private airport in Nevers. It landed to a tremendous reception from my staff and volunteers, the media, helpers and well-wishers. Forty dogs were brought to the *Refuge de Thiernay*, some to be rehomed in France, the others through my animal welfare contacts in Germany and Switzerland.

I had visited the Crete shelter in 1995 and felt so sorry for the dogs. Although they had plenty of space and were clearly well fed, they were desperate for affection and climbed over one another to push their heads against the wire of their enclosures in hopes of a friendly gesture or kind word. Most of them had never lived in a home and many had been at the Crete shelter for years, so we had to carefully select prospective adopters relying on the accuracy of each of the dogs' psychological profiles.

Moving animals from one country to another is not the answer to the unwanted dog problem, but neither is a shelter in a remote location. It reinforced my belief that although shelters have a role to play in the rehoming process, ideally they should only be used for short-term measures. Dogs are sociable creatures that thrive in the security of a caring home and can easily become 'kennel crazy' if kept in a shelter too long – indeed, it is similar to a prison sentence. The current president of GAWF, Brian Cowie and the Council of Management, agree with these sentiments and now focus on educational activities and provide grants to help the work of other organisations in Greece.

In keeping with GAWF's educational strategy, in May 1997 David organised the first animal welfare seminar at Thessaloniki University's Faculty of Veterinary Medicine. It was held over two days with high profile presenters and I was honoured to be the guest speaker and open the seminar.

Château Chimps: France

I cannot bear the thought of wild animals being kept as pets in a domestic setting, so when I learned of a château about 50 kilometres from my Refuge that had several wild animals, I immediately wanted to find out more. It was the year 2000, the twenty-first century, so why were we still keeping wild animals in this way in France?

I discovered that the owner of the château had died and her children were in the process of selling the house and could not agree on what to do with the animals. They were thinking about sending them to laboratories or zoos in other countries, but the caretakers of the château who had looked after the animals did not want this to happen, as the chimpanzees were used to going into the house and sitting at the table for their food!

2003. With David van Gennep (Stichting AAP) during the relocation of chimps from a Château in France to AAP Centre in Holland.

Credit: David Barnes/AAP

162

I knew I had to find a solution so I contacted David Barnes, who has helped me many times at the Refuge and has also successfully relocated exotic animals from unsuitable facilities in Greece. He immediately agreed to help and came to France to visit the château with me and discuss what could be done for the animals. When we arrived we learned that the caretaker wanted to take some of the birds and some small monkeys to live at his home. It was not ideal, but at least he knew the animals and wanted to care for them, so part of the problem was resolved.

However, three chimpanzees needed to be relocated – an adult male, a female and their one-year-old baby. The male had grown very large and aggressive and was almost 30 kg over the average weight for a male chimp – the average chimp weight being about 45 kg. David, always practical and resourceful, immediately contacted the Dutch organisation, *Stichting AAP*, who have excellent facilities for apes in Almere, but more importantly they have knowledgeable staff who assess the animals and provide specifically for their individual needs. David had worked with them when rescuing monkeys from Crete and mainland Greece, so he knew that they were the best people to help us find the right homes for the chimps.

AAP agreed to help and a few weeks later the AAP wildlife team with their director David van Gennep drove from the Netherlands to France with a film crew. They were making a documentary on AAP and were delighted to include the rescue of chimpanzees from a French château.

The chimpanzees had to be heavily sedated before loading them into their transportation crates and the large male was the first to be sedated. One of the AAP team used a blowpipe to shoot a tranquillising dart into him and thankfully the large animal went to sleep quickly without any fuss.

Next it was the female's turn to be darted but this did not go so smoothly. She was desperately trying to protect her baby so the sedative took much longer to have the desired effect. At last she was loaded into the crate but recovered from the sedation almost immediately; she was so angry at being separated from her baby, and aggressively showed just *how* angry!

The next five minutes were most disturbing for both humans and animals as the team tried in vain to catch the extremely fast baby chimpanzee, but eventually he was caught and put into the crate with his mother. They were both so relieved to be together again and settled down for the long drive back to Holland.

There needs to be more public awareness of keeping wild animals where they belong – in the wild. Why does man feel the need to possess and dominate wild animals?

Before their return, the film crew interviewed me as they were curious to know why I had chosen to spend my life helping animals and why I had never married. I explained that somehow I felt responsible for animals in France, so I was extremely thankful to David Barnes and *Stichting AAP* for giving these chimpanzees a brighter future. Also I have never found the time, or the need to be married and although there have been many charming men in my life, there has always been many more animals that needed my time and love.

9

The Tide is Turning

Farm Animal Welfare

As I was born and bred in a rural location in the centre of France, I have always been comfortable around farm animals especially cattle, as my family have a long tradition in the breeding of Charolais. They originated in central France in the areas of Charolles and Nièvre and although there is speculation as to the exact origins of the breed, legend tells of white cattle in the region as early as 878 AD. By the sixteenth and seventeenth centuries these cattle were popular in French markets.

In 1773 Claude Mathieu, a farmer and cattle producer from the Charolles region, moved to the Nièvre region, taking his herd of white cattle with him which he bred with the local white cattle. The offspring were called Charolais. My great-great-great grandfather Brière d'Azy was one of the early breeders of the Charolais and crossed his white cattle with the British Durham Shorthorn.

My sister Mimi decided early in life that she too wanted to be a farmer and breed Charolais cattle, so my parents acted as guarantors for her and Mimi took out a loan to buy a farm and two cows. From these cows she established one of the finest breeding Charolais herds in France; 200 head of cattle, with many that won the major championship show competitions in France. Although Mimi was slimly-built and lean-bodied throughout her life, she did all the manual work on her farm and was strong and fearless. She ploughed the fields with draught horses, then bought a tractor and the first combine harvester in the region.

Mimi, who sadly died in 2003, lived and farmed at Mânoir de

1962. John MacFarlane showing me the humane stun guns brought by him
to France from the USA.

Credit: Studio Rosardy, 122 Rue la Boëtie, Paris

Valotte, a fifteenth-century farmhouse about 3 kilometres from *Refuge de Thiernay*. The grounds are surrounded by high gates with sharp pointed spikes put there in the seventeenth century to prevent the wolves getting in with the sheep and cattle. Mimi became well known for her expertise with cattle and for the quality of her stock and was one of the first people in France to export Charolais to the UK after World War II. As her reputation spread, she was invited to judge at agricultural shows and advise the farming industry in many countries, including Canada, Thailand, Brazil and the USA. She was decorated for her services to French agriculture.

I too was interested in farm animals, but mainly from the animal welfare perspective, including methods of slaughter, which were of major concern to me. In the early 1960s it was not obligatory in French abattoirs to stun animals before slaughtering and there were no humane stun guns in France. But this all changed when Madame Jacqueline Gilardoni became aware of the harsh realities for animals in abattoirs and the inhumane methods of slaughter. Her crusade began in 1957 when an old donkey escaped from a slaughterhouse and was cared for by her daughter Eve. This donkey was to become the symbol for all the animals that were abused and sacrificed in abattoirs in France and was the catalyst for Madame Gilardoni's long active life of dedication for the humane treatment of animals in abattoirs.

She became so concerned for the animals sent for slaughter that she often went into the abattoirs illegally so she could see at first hand what was actually happening and to collect further information for her dossier. She then started to campaign for the humane treatment of animals sent for slaughter and made contact with people in other countries – especially in the UK – for help and advice.

In 1961, Dr André Triau, a friend of mine, encouraged Madame Gilardoni to set up an organisation, *Œuvre d'Assistance aux Bêtes d'Abattoirs* (*l'OABA*), to give credibility for her cause and she soon gained the support of the veterinary profession. She organised a petition demanding humane slaughter equipment and legislation to control methods of slaughter in abattoirs, which soon had more than 150,000 signatures, including those of media personalities such as Edith Piaf. Dr Fernand Méry, a wonderful compassionate veterinarian

Campaigning with PMAF and HSI in France.

Credit: RdeT collection

who motivated animal welfarists in France, supported this action with editorial and radio broadcasts.

Through her overseas advisors, Madame Gilardoni contacted the Massachusetts Society for the Prevention of Cruelty to Animals (MSPCA), in Boston, USA and in 1962, their Vice-President of Agricultural Education, John MacFarlane, brought the first humane stun guns to France, sponsored by the International Society for the Protection of Animals (ISPA).

Madame Gilardoni asked me if I would meet John MacFarlane and arrange publicity with the media. I did as she asked and received the humane stunners from John at a lively meeting with journalists, who asked many questions, and were fascinated to learn about the humane equipment. Reluctantly, I had to leave John in the afternoon as I was going to the Belgian Embassy to a reception in honour of Queen Elisabeth of Belgium. When I arrived carrying the guns, the same journalists and photographers who by now had arrived at the embassy hoping to photograph Queen Elisabeth, were most amused to find that I had taken the guns to the reception. The following

168

day the newspapers showed the arrival of the humane stunners in France with me meeting Mr MacFarlane. Then they showed me arriving at the Belgian Embassy for the reception, carrying the guns!

In 1964 the Minister of Agriculture signed a decree for the humane slaughter of animals in abattoirs throughout France and later, in 1970, extended this directive to include the humane slaughter of poultry and rabbits. Madame Gilardoni died in 2001 aged eighty-six, but her work lives on as *l'OABA* under the direction of Dr Jean-Pierre Kieffer, a dedicated veterinarian in Paris. It continues to investigate and monitor farms and markets, also the transport of animals and abattoirs procedures to make sure that regulations are being observed. Two hundred surveys were carried out last year.

Following my visit to Udaipur in 1976, Annabella Singh and I became close friends and regularly exchanged information and opinions on animal welfare issues. Both of us were painfully aware of the numerous issues in India, such as the poaching of wild animals, the appalling zoos, and the street shows using monkeys, snakes, and bears. We were especially concerned for farm animals as we had been told

1992. In my kitchen with Utopique a rescue horse, who regularly came in for an apple!

Credit: Jon Bradley

that the treatment of animals in the slaughterhouses and methods used for slaughter were simply appalling. So we decided to do some research and made plans to assess the situation at a slaughterhouse in Delhi.

In 1981 I travelled to India again to stay with Annabella at the Udaipur City Palace and a few days later we went together to Delhi by bus, a journey of about eight hours. Annabella had already made arrangements for us to visit a Delhi slaughterhouse on two consecutive days, a most unusual request, especially from two ladies. The first day was to observe how the animals were transported and unloaded and the second day was to watch the animals being slaughtered and to record the methods of handling and slaughter. We were outside the slaughterhouse early in the morning, in time for the first arrivals of goats and cattle.

The lorries started arriving, several were open-topped vehicles with animals lurching against each other as they tried to keep their balance. We stayed in the background to avoid suspicion and watched as the first lorry unloaded the animals. There were no unloading ramps and the goats inside were bundled together with their legs tied and were carelessly hurled from the lorry, crashing in a heap on to the ground below. Their screams echoed through the air as they cried out in pain and terror.

The cattle were treated in a similar callous manner as several men beat them hard with sticks and brooms, forcing them off the back of the lorry. As the cattle crashed to the ground we could hear limbs crack and shatter. Many of the goats and the cattle were either unable to get up, or to walk, but instead of helping the animals, the men appeared from inside the slaughterhouse and began beating them with sticks. The animals that could not stand were kicked aggressively and dragged into the slaughterhouse. The animals which did stagger into the slaughterhouse had to negotiate concrete steps, but in their panic lost their footing and tripped over each other, so were again subjected to more kicking and beating. What appalling misery and pain for these poor animals!

The following day we returned to the slaughterhouse and went inside to watch the actual slaughter procedures. We watched in silence as the beautiful cattle were 'attacked' by the slaughtermen. There was no restraint or stunning for the cattle, just frenzied attacks by the workers, literally leaping at the terrified animals with knives ready to slit their throats. The noise was deafening as the animals bellowed in pain. Many broke away from the attacks of the slaughtermen and rushed around with blood spurting from their throats.

It was a dangerous place to be as there appeared to be little, if any, control of the animals or indeed the slaughtermen. Sadly amongst all this danger and horror, there were numerous children running around watching the spectacle, seeming to enjoy the chaos, oblivious to the brutality of the men and suffering of the animals.

We made our way to the manager's office, wading through blood, guts, urine and faeces, the stench overpowering our senses. We dared not slip on the reddish-brown matter under our feet, as we desperately tried to walk steadily and appear to be composed, although our hearts were crying. We were both smartly dressed as we were having lunch with Monsieur Ross, the French Ambassador and his wife, following this visit. What a strange sight in a slaughterhouse, a maharani in a green and gold silk sari and a European princess in a Dior dress, trying to be dignified picking our path through stinking pools of the remains of dead animals and other waste matter!

The manager was uncouth and uninterested in our concerns. I tried to explain that the slaughtermen could be trained to handle the animals more effectively and therefore reduce potential injury for both humans and animals; also improved animal management could save manpower and time and generally improve efficiency of the slaughterhouse. They could also address the problems with contaminated meat, as it was not separated from meat for human consumption. He replied: 'So what!' I remember his words so clearly. We left his office with heavy hearts, still in shock at what we had seen and in despair at his indifferent and uncaring attitude.

We related the whole scenario to the ambassador and his wife, pouring out the gruesome details of our visit to the slaughterhouse, while they listened intently, hardly able to take in the full horror of the situation. They vowed that they would never buy meat in India again, but in future would have it imported from Paris.

We decided to write a report for WSPA and also gave full details to the Prime Minister of India, Indira Gandhi, when we met her at the Convention on International Trade in Endangered Species (CITES) meeting in Delhi. At the meeting we were shown an enchanting film on native birds of India. However my mind kept straying to the appalling abuse of animals at the slaughterhouse in Delhi, the cries of the goats, the screaming and moaning of the cattle, the stench and the children watching, unperturbed.

I have been to slaughterhouses in other countries: in the UK, France and the Philippines. Fortunately, none of the visits has been as traumatic as the visit to the Delhi slaughterhouse, although none in my opinion are pleasant places to visit.

The abuse and cruelty towards farm animals are the biggest animal welfare problems in the world when we consider the numbers of animals affected, yet there are still only a few animal welfare organisations set up to specifically focus on farm animals. One is Compassion in World Farming (CIWF) in the UK, a dynamic organisation which gets results. Their small team of staff is led by Phil Lymbery, ably supported by John Callaghan and Joyce d'Silva, all seasoned campaigners. John is a great favourite of mine and it has always amused him that I once described him as a 'man of quality', but this expression describes him perfectly as he truly is a loyal friend to people and animals.

I have followed the work of CIWF for about twenty-five years and was delighted when they extended their remit and helped to establish a sister organisation in France in 1994, *Protection Mondiale des Animaux de Ferme* (*PMAF*) based in Metz, in the Moselle region.

CIWF was set up in 1967 by dairy farmer Peter Roberts and his wife Anna to campaign against factory farming and the welfare concerns associated with long-distance transport and slaughter of farm animals. At the time, few people in the UK seemed to care about the treatment of farm animals and Peter Roberts was ridiculed for his attempts to get animal sentiency recognised in law. After all, farm animals were only bred to be killed and eaten! Yet in 1997 after thirty years of campaigning, the EU agreed to legally recognise farm animals as 'sentient beings'. This was a great victory for the status of animals throughout Europe, as it recognised that they can suffer and that future legislation must take this into account.

The founders of *Protection Mondiale des Animaux de Ferme* (*PMAF*) in France were Ghislain Zuccolo who became the first Director of *PMAF* and Charles Notin, who took on the role as President. Before establishing *PMAF*, Ghislain spent a year working at CIWF UK, to learn how the organisation functioned, with a focus on their campaigns and lobbying. He realised that some methods of working, although effective in the UK, would have to be modified and repackaged, as the French way of life and attitudes were very different. Although the countries of France and the UK are in close proximity geographically, they have wide cultural differences on many issues. Farming has traditionally been seen as a way of life in France, not just as a job or an activity, but as a right to be pursued as the individual chooses without interference from others. Lobbying is seen as a British activity, but viewed with suspicion in France as French people are more inclined to take to the streets and demonstrate.

France has always been an important country with regard to the transport of farm animals, as animals travel long distances through France, such as from Holland to Spain and from Ireland to Greece. Although there is legislation in place to protect these animals, in the past it has been largely ignored. *PMAF* now goes out with the motorway police several times a year and does spot checks on animals in transit, using a checklist which they circulate to the 4,000 police stations throughout France.

About fifteen years ago I went to Finland with my friend Amelia to look at the ways in which the Scandinavian countries transport animals. The interior of the transport lorries was so well designed with separate compartments for the animals depending on their type, size and sex. Immaculately clean, the lorries had automatic watering facilities, isolation facilities and air conditioning. Also the drivers and animal handlers were specifically trained for their respective roles. If only other countries would adopt similar practices.

Through my charity's magazine, I give coverage of CIWF and *PMAF*'s work as often as I can. *PMAF* now has eight employees and 13,000 supporters and although CIWF still provide support for some projects, the work is done entirely by French employees and volunteers.

Recently, *PMAF* exhibited the work of their organisation at the *Salon de l'Agriculture* in Paris, a large agricultural show attracting 700,000 people. *PMAF* used the opportunity to try to increase awareness of the welfare issues involved with battery-produced eggs, in contrast to the production of free-range eggs.

The response from the public was overwhelming, which shows clearly how attitudes towards the welfare of farm animals are changing in France. When *PMAF* started their work seventeen years ago, only 2% of the public chose to buy free-range eggs, compared with 20% now. *PMAF* is making a big difference in France, as indeed CIWF is doing in the UK and Peter Roberts' vision of humane methods of farming is gradually becoming a reality.

Horses have always been one of my great loves. My father bred them and we kept several at Château d'Azy as general riding horses and my life up until I left home in my early twenties included almost daily rides around the countryside of the Nièvre. My sisters, brother and I, all became competent riders at an early age as we were put in the saddle almost from birth.

My cousin Charles, the Head of the House of Croÿ at his family seat in Dülmen, owns the only herd of wild ponies in Germany and the ponies, simply known as the Dülmeners, have been in the same area since the early 1300s. There are about 400 roaming wild over 860 acres of the Merfelder Bruch area of Dülmen, where there is a wide diversity of habitat ranging from woodland to open moorland, providing every environment the ponies may need depending on the climatic conditions. The ponies, which stand around twelve to thirteen hands, are left to live wild so they have to forage for their food, find shelter and cope with disease or illness without intervention, so only the strongest survive as in a typical wild situation. Only in extreme weather conditions are they given hay, if the ground and bushes are frozen.

Once a year on the last Saturday in May, the ponies are rounded up and the colts separated from the herd. Just one or two stallions are left with the mares, with the colts sold at public auction as they make suitable children's ponies or driving ponies. Thousands of people attend the auction, not necessarily to buy a pony, but to see so many ponies rounded up each year is an amazing spectacle and the free spirit of the wild ponies is a delight to witness.

In contrast, most of the large horse sales held in France are a miserable experience to witness, as any equine unlucky enough to end up at one of these markets is likely to be sold for slaughter, mainly for human consumption but also for their skins and for dog food.

In 2000 I went to a sale in Maurs in the Cantal region of Central France, about 300 kilometres from the *Refuge de Thiernay*, where there were 3,000 horses and donkeys for sale. At the time we had space at the Refuge for a couple of rescue horses so we hired a large horse box and a friend, Jerome Young, drove another friend and me, to the horse market at Maurs.

Many of the horses at the sale were in very poor condition with scabby coats, snotty noses, desperately thin bodies, and feet seriously overgrown with split hooves. Some animals were just too weary to show any reaction to the poking and prodding by prospective owners, while others stamped and snorted rebelliously. Young, wide-eyed foals quivered and shook in sheer fright while their mothers tried to protect them from the heavy hands of some of the spectators by lunging wildly with bared teeth and kicking aggressively. Representatives from the then Paris-based World Equine Organisation and the UK Donkey Sanctuary were there closely monitoring the conditions and treatment and I knew they would report their concerns to the authorities who regulate the sales.

We bought seven animals including a pathetic-looking white donkey that was lying down, probably to relieve the pain of standing on his elongated, curled-up hooves; a large thin draught horse, simply because the owner was so persistent and a beautiful mare that was so thin, with a profuse nasal discharge. Jerome also bought a white male donkey. The thin mare ended up living with Jerome and once on the road to recovery was transformed into a beautiful creature. Jerome's donkey eventually came to live at *Refuge de Thiernay*, the other white donkey went to a private rescue home and the draught horse lived at the Refuge for about seven weeks when he suddenly fell down one day and never got up again – at least he had a few weeks of peace and love.

Tragedy of the Circus

The circus spectacle has been in existence since the days of ancient Rome when thousands of people attended organised entertainment which featured the use of animals, mainly elephants, horses and lions.

The slaves were forced to fight off the hungry lions and if any of the slaves survived, then he might be given his freedom.

The circus as we know it today seems to have started in the eighteenth century in Europe and gradually spread throughout the world. Yet the immense suffering of animals which are kept in circuses specifically to 'entertain' humans has only really become known in the past fifteen years and there is still limited legislation to give protection to these animals.

In 1990 Animal Defenders International (ADI) was founded by Jan Creamer in the UK and for the past twenty-three years she has been the Chief Executive Officer. Together with Tim Phillips, the Campaigns Director and a small team, they have done exceptional work with in-depth investigations, highlighting such issues as animals used in circuses and other forms of entertainment and wild animals kept as pets. I have known Jan and Tim for more than ten years and find their educational publications most informative and whenever I hear of a circus where there are animals I try to find out what's going on and report to ADI.

Jan and Tim live and breathe animal protection. At their home after work they treat local wild foxes that have mange with honey sandwiches dosed with a homeopathic remedy – a hugely successful treatment. I printed a picture in our magazine of their garden swarming with foxes when a vixen brought her cubs to visit; perhaps a reward for their kindness; a reminder of the joy compassion can bring.

Traditionally in France, cabaret acts performed at places such as the Moulin Rouge and the Lido in Paris have used animals on stage to 'entertain'. We have often received complaints at the *Refuge de Thiernay* from concerned people who have seen the acts, but other than making representation to the local authorities, who invariably appear to be indifferent to animal abuse, there is little more we can do as we have our own priorities which takes up all our time and energy. Sadly, animals are still used in cabaret acts and circuses still travel throughout France, giving performances to 'entertain' the public, many of whom have little knowledge or understanding of the shocking treatment used to 'train' and 'condition' these captive wild animals.

France is not the only country, as circuses travel throughout Europe (and the rest of the world), although fewer than in the past, as more and more are now opting to have human acrobatic acts instead of animal acts, thanks to the exposure and pressure of groups such as ADI.

I have been to only a few circuses in my life, but I have seen enough live animal acts and abhor the entire concept – the thought of how the animals are confined and trained is distressing to contemplate. About twelve years ago I helped to investigate the living quarters of animals in a circus in Greece for a veterinarian who was preparing a report; some of the animals could hardly turn round in their boxes and large animals such as the elephant and rhino were tethered by heavy chains around their legs and could only move a distance of a few feet.

About thirty years ago I went to a circus in Moscow and although some of the details are hazy now, I can clearly recall a bizarre act where a glamorous lady swept into the arena, wearing a full-length fur coat. She swaggered around for about two minutes with the coat extravagantly swinging from side to side – then stopped and sharply clapped her hands. At that point, the 'fur coat' fell to pieces and hundreds, perhaps thousands, of live rats fell to the ground and scuttled out of the arena!

Between 1996 and 1998, Animal Defenders International conducted a remarkable undercover investigation of the circus industry. ADI Field Officers took jobs in circuses and training centres throughout the UK and parts of Europe, gathering evidence on video of how circus animals were trained. The shocking images of animals being relentlessly beaten confirmed what they had always suspected, that these animals were not trained with kindness and reward, but with violence and intimidation. Within months of the exposé, half the British circuses with animals had closed down and the evidence sent a shock wave around the world leading to circus prohibitions as far afield as Singapore and Rio de Janiero.

An elephant keeper was jailed for his repeated attacks on the elephants in his care, and in 1999 ADI took Chipperfield, the most famous name in animal circuses, to court. Mary Chipperfield of the legendary circus family was convicted of thrashing and beating Trudy, a young chimpanzee. Yet under oath, Chipperfield maintained she'd done nothing wrong as it was 'good animal husbandry' and it was

2002. Toto the chimpanzee lived alone in a wooden packing case which was little more than a metre wide. He was kept in chains at Chile's Circus Konig, where he had lived for twenty years. Toto was rescued by ADI and taken to a sanctuary in Africa where he joined a family of other chimpanzees.

Credit: Animal Defenders International

2003. Toto with his new family at the Chimfunshi Wildlife Orphanage, Zambia.

Credit: Animal Defenders International

1996. Elephants chained at the Monte Carlo Circus Festival – sadly a typical sight at circuses around the world.

Credit: Animal Defenders International

no different from the way she treated her own children – even though video evidence showed her beating the small chimp with a stick and kicking her in the back and side of her body. Chipperfield and her husband Roger Cawley, who, at the time was a British zoo inspector, were both convicted of cruelty; he for repeatedly whipping a sick elephant. The chimpanzee, Trudy, was placed in a sanctuary and the huge UK multi-million pound base of Mary Chipperfield Promotions closed down.

Thanks to ADI bringing this high-profile court case, the treatment of animals in circuses was truly in the spotlight; it was the first ever conviction against a major animal trainer.

The repercussions continued. During the investigation, my friend Tim had worked undercover for Dicky Chipperfield, Mary's cousin at another establishment, Chipperfield Enterprises. This was Europe's biggest training centre for lions and tigers. Chipperfield had trained over 1,000 lions and tigers which were sold or rented, and they appeared in circuses all over the continent. As the ADI footage of these poor, magnificent animals being beaten and living in metal shipping containers emerged, the business collapsed and within a few years was closed. Dicky Chipperfield did not give up. Instead, he headed to France to continue training – and, that was where I came in. In 2003 we tracked him down to Circus Jean Richard Pinder. I would help by calling ahead to find out where the circus was and finding volunteers to scout out where animals were being kept and which animals were present. Then the ADI team moved in and secretly filmed Dicky Chipperfield training, shouting at the proud beasts and striking them to subdue them. At one point on the video, he was threatening '*I'll sort you*' and repeatedly swearing, and then hit a tiger in the face with a metal pole.

My collaboration with ADI tracking circuses in Europe continued for years and I was delighted when they expanded their operations to South America.

They began with the rescue of a dear chimpanzee called Toto from a circus in Chile. He was being forced to live alone in a packing crate for over twenty years, was forced to smoke cigarettes to amuse people, and had had his teeth torn out to stop him defending himself. ADI went through the courts to save him and then took him all the way home to Africa, from where he had been stolen as baby. After two decades in isolation he embraced another chimpanzee again and Tim and Jan told me how their eyes filled with tears as the two chimps clung to each other not wanting to let go.

I had travelled through South America and was aware of terrible animal suffering especially in zoos and circuses and would call Tim asking if ADI could help. It is a relatively small organisation but he would always say: '*We'll see what we can do if we have someone in the area.*' He was as good as his word. ADI put a team of Field Officers into the South American circus industry where they gathered information and video. They stayed undercover in this horrible and dangerous environment for over two years, eventually collecting evidence of cruelty in circuses in Bolivia, Brazil, Chile, Colombia, Ecuador, and Peru.

When the findings were released it made headlines throughout the continent. In Colombia, a poor chimpanzee called Karla who was punched in the face and beaten with a chain, became a focus of public anger at the circus.

ADI turned the exposé into a drive for legislation and two years later in May 2009, Bolivia became the first South American country to ban the use of animals in circuses. At the same time legislation to ban animal circuses has been progressing through the parliaments of Peru and Brazil and awaits a vote in Congress. Legislation to ban animal circuses is currently before the governments of Colombia, Greece, Norway and the UK is discussing regulation to prohibit wild animals. Prohibitions have already been secured in thousands of towns and cities, including my nearest town Nevers, as well as nationally in Austria, Croatia, Hungary, Singapore and Costa Rica. The tide is indeed turning.

Another global ADI campaign is 'My Mate's a Primate', where it highlights all aspects of primates used for entertainment and wild animals kept as pets. The following extracts from the 'My Mate's a Primate' report explain the misery of the circus for the 'entertainers', and the full publication gives a harrowing account of how we treat our closest relatives.

Worldwide, many different primate species are used in entertainment.

181

This includes advertising, films, television and circus shows. In circus acts currently touring chimps are dressed in clothes, ride bicycles, roller blade and simulate playing the guitar; baboons dressed in nappies walk a tightrope, push a scooter and use a slide, baboons and monkeys are chained to ponies in order to ride them around the ring. In advertising apes are dressed as people, pretend to drive cars, fall over as if drunk and 'grin' at the camera. In fact the chimpanzee's 'grin' we so often see is an expression of fear. Our entertainers are compelled to do almost everything except act natural.

There is no justification for the use of primates in any form of entertainment. The cost to the individual animals is enormous; isolation from their own kind, never to be touched by someone who understands them, irreparable psychological damage and a lifetime of loneliness. In order to literally break these animals' desire for independence and free will they are beaten, malnourished, mutilated, isolated and caged.

The following extract describes the effect on primates kept as pets:

Monkeys and apes are wild animals who cannot be domesticated and who will inevitably suffer from the restrictions of life as a pet. They will be denied the opportunity to display the normal social, physiological and psychological behaviours typical of their species. Even the most well-meaning owner cannot provide for the wide spectrum of needs essential to a healthy primate. The trade in primates is often illicit, involves cruelty and suffering in the capture, breeding, dealing and so often the keeping of these intelligent and complex animals. The welfare and conservation of wild and captive primates are compromised by the trade, which also poses serious health threats to the human population.

'My Mate's a Primate' quotes: '*Just as we are ashamed of what our ancestors have done to people who were considered to be different from us, by exploiting them as slaves or as children in our factories, so too some day will our children be ashamed of what we do today to our sibling species, the chimpanzee.*'

182

The area of animal experiments is perhaps where primates suffer the most and ADI have led a Europe-wide drive to end the suffering of apes and monkeys in laboratories as part of the campaign. In 2007 they launched an ambitious Written Declaration before the European Parliament calling for an end to the use of great apes and wild-caught monkeys in experiments and for a timetable to be established to phase out all experiments on monkeys. They needed the signatures of half the members of the parliament to make this a resolution, but had just four months to do it. The ADI team began walking the corridors of power in Brussels and Strasbourg, addressing meetings, publishing reports in many languages, and slowly gathering signatures. They called in all their friends to help. At the *Refuge de Thiernay* during plenary sessions of the European Parliament the fax would run hot as we sent messages to MEPs urging them to sign. I would call MEPs asking them to at least consider the proposal, to read the latest information, and to please sign. And, slowly they did.

In September 2007, support for the ADI Written Declaration surged past the required 50% reaching a staggering 433 signatures and was adopted by the European Parliament. The Declaration that many claimed could not succeed, turned out to be the third highest supported Declaration in the Parliament and the best ever supported on animal protection. We had pulled together and won. It was issued as an instruction to the European Commission for new rules on laboratory experiments.

In late 2008, the Commission proposed new rules for animal experiments across Europe banning the use of wild-caught monkeys in experiments, prohibiting the use of apes except in extraordinary circumstances and phase out the wild capture of monkeys by laboratory breeding centres over seven years. In 2009 these are being discussed by the European Parliament where an ADI amendment for a bi-annual review to set targets for replacement of all monkey experiments has already been adopted. There is huge opposition from the wealthy research industry and the proposals are unlikely to be adopted unscathed. But the tide is starting to turn here, too.

The work and findings of ADI need to be heard throughout the world so that younger generations will understand the misery of animals used in entertainment and kept as pets. In the reception area of the *Refuge de Thiernay* office, we have posters showing the work of ADI and write about them in our magazine. I know this is just small exposure for such immense suffering, but we can all do something to influence and educate others about these issues. For example, so many adults and children when seeing a smiling, performing chimp simply do not understand that the poor animal is crying inside. So, let them know, don't hold back out of 'politeness'.

I recently read the following statement in an article published in 1931 by a well-known magazine: '*Geographically, the circus has been a great educator.*' The article was glorifying the circus and the spectacle of man dominating animals. I shuddered, thinking not only of the animals that have suffered appalling abuse through the years, but also the human beings, exploited through the circus 'freak shows'. What an education!

How times are changing! Through the work of organisations such as ADI we are no longer bamboozled by spangles and sawdust, but can now see clearly the degradation of the circus and the cruel exploitation of both humans and animals. Promise me you will *never* go to a circus!

10

Influence and Inspiration

So many people, events and activities have inspired me through the years, sometimes just for a short period, but others have made such an impression that the effect has lasted forever. I mentioned in an earlier chapter that ballet and art have always been a source of beauty and inspiration for me and a visit to the theatre or to a museum can be guaranteed to boost my flagging spirits. Although my early life was shaped mainly by my father and my Aunt Marie, I continue to be influenced and inspired by kind actions from people who are simply doing their everyday job.

A few years ago I was in a street in Paris, heavily laden with bags of donated goods collected for Romania, and I was trying to get a taxi. The streets were in chaos as there was a rail strike and all the taxis were taken. Suddenly I saw a taxi start to weave through the traffic and head towards me. What a relief! The young driver jumped from his cab and put all my bags into his vehicle, then politely helped me climb into the passenger seat.

He asked me why I was carrying so many large bags and packages. I explained that I collected unwanted clothes and other useful items to send to countries in Eastern Europe. We immediately struck up a rapport and I learned overtime that he, David Tang, was now forty and that he and his family had left Cambodia in the 1970s. In just four years in his home country, the Khmer Rouge regime executed, starved and worked to death up to two million people as their leader Pol Pot systematically tried to create a peasant society by emptying the cities of educated people and forcing them to work in the fields. The atrocities in Cambodia were one of the worst mass killings of the twentieth century. Although the lives of David and his family

2000. David Tang at a Buddhist Temple in Myanmar.

Credit: David Tang

were disrupted for several years, he has no bitterness towards the oppressors.

He has a beautiful soul and is a true Buddhist in word and deed and refuses to accept payment for any taxi journeys for charitable purposes and even gives donations to some of his passengers. When Betty Wang and Shen Cheng from China briefly visited my Refuge in 2005, David collected them from the airport, took them on a sightseeing tour of Paris and then to the train station for their journey to Nevers. He knew that Betty and Shen Cheng were travelling on a limited budget and were in Europe to attend the 'Pioneer' animal welfare course in Italy so he refused to accept any payment, although he had used a day of his time and showed such kindness to those two young people, whom he had not met before and may never see again. Just one simple example of David's love for humanity.

Others who have inspired me over the years and whose influence continues to inspire me, include André Malraux; Wu Hung; John Walsh; Christine Stevens and Mother Teresa. Of course there are others who have influenced me in a negative way, but fortunately any such influence has been short-lived and is in the past, never to be revived.

André Malraux

I was fortunate to become acquainted with André Malraux, the author, adventurer and influential figure in French politics and culture, during the early 1960s after we met at the Belgian Embassy where we had an interesting discussion about the Croÿ family history, which he seemed to know better than I did.

We immediately struck up a friendship and became firm friends, even though he was more than twenty years older than me. He was already a very busy well-known public figure and I found him a most fascinating man because whatever subject came up in conversation, he could converse with such knowledge and authority. He was such a cultured person and seemed to be on a different plane to most people, also I greatly admired his adventurous spirit and capacity for getting things done. In addition to his travels and his demanding

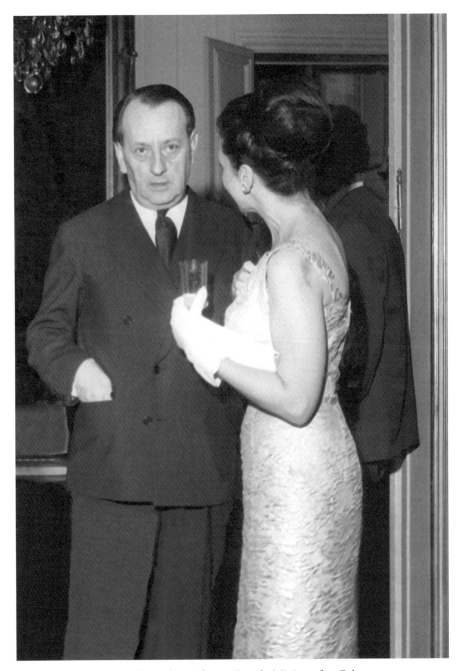

1964. With André Malraux, French Minister for Culture.

Credit: R. Delhay, 30. Avenue Aristide-Briand 30, Stains (Seine), C.C.C. Paris

government position, he still found the time to write numerous published books and articles.

He was adventurous from a young age and in 1923 when only twenty-one he made an expedition into the jungles of Cambodia to find the hidden temples and re-discovered the temple known as the Banteay Srei, originally discovered in 1914.

When World War II began, he joined the French Army but was captured the following year. He escaped and joined the French Resistance but was eventually captured by the Gestapo in 1944. After the end of the war, Malraux became the Minister for Information and was later appointed the first Minister of Culture.

I learned a lot about life from Malraux especially how one must develop a defence mechanism when faced with adversity. His life was marred by tragedy with several members of his family killed in unrelated accidents, including his second wife and his two sons.

When he died in 1976 his two cats, Fourrure and Lustre, came to live with me at the Refuge. Before meeting Malraux I had never met anyone quite like him and I have never met anyone quite like him since.

John Walsh

John Walsh is a great man I have known for about thirty-five years and the former International Projects Director of WSPA. On many occasions I've attended WSPA meetings and listened in awe to accounts of John's activities and bravery, rescuing animals from so many disaster areas around the world such as the Kobe earthquake in Japan; the volcano eruption in Montserrat and the war in Bosnia, to name just a few of his exploits. His avid interest and encyclopaedic knowledge on all animal-related matters is legendary and his influence on so many young colleagues he has trained cannot be underestimated. Known as a hard taskmaster, he would only accept 100% effort and woe betide anyone who fell short.

John, who retired in 2004, was a giant in every sense of the word, standing well over six feet, handsome, broad-shouldered, fast talking, outspoken and fearless in his quest to tackle animal cruelty and abuse.

2000. With John Walsh, WSPA International Projects Director, at a WSPA
fundraising event in London.

Credit: WSPA

1995. With Master Wu Hung at *Refuge de Thiernay.*

Credit: RdeT collection

Indeed, he was every bit the James Bond of the animal welfare world; a man of action. I greatly admired John as nothing was impossible for him. His enthusiasm was infectious as he believed something could always be done to improve a situation and he always made time to relate to local people in a country, so he could understand their traditions and cultural beliefs. A rare jewel!

Wu Hung

Wu Hung is an exceptional person in every way. He was a Buddhist monk when I first met him and was also the Secretary General of LCA, Taiwan. From the very first moment I saw him waiting serenely at the airport in Taipei, I knew he was special in a spiritual sense. His gentle persona has a calming influence on me whenever we meet and even when I think about him. He is such a courageous person challenging so many rituals with animals and attitudes towards animals in Asia and tirelessly works as a volunteer leader for the Environment and Animal Society Taiwan, known as EAST, the organisation he founded in 1999.

About ten years ago he was heavily criticised in Taiwan for his outspoken views on animal abuse, his challenging of religious traditions and attitudes, his support of humane euthanasia for animals in extreme circumstances, his campaign for humane treatment of animals in slaughterhouses and his opposition to animals in circuses. It was considered wrong by many of his countrymen for a Buddhist monk to speak out publicly on these issues, and even his own colleagues distanced themselves from his views and opinions. Very much his own man, Wu Hung has proved to be a true pioneer and now commands respect worldwide for his selfless and compassionate attitude to human, animal and environmental welfare.

Christine Stevens

Christine Stevens was the founder of the Animal Welfare Institute in the USA in 1951 and led the organisation until her death in 2002.

1994. With Christine Stevens, founder of the Animal Welfare Institute, Washington DC, USA.

Credit: RdeT collection

She was a powerful voice speaking out against many issues including the cruel treatment of animals in laboratories, factory farming, commercial whaling, the leg-hold trap, the extinction of endangered species and the killing of great apes for bushmeat. I first met her many years ago at a meeting of the European Parliament in Strasbourg. I can't remember exactly when, but I remember we were instantly drawn to each other and developed a warm relationship. I found her to be such an inspirational lady with an aura of tranquillity which always impressed me as I struggle at times to maintain my own dignity when confronted with issues of cruelty and abuse. Christine was a person who appeared to be in control of her emotions at all times; a great asset in her work. In the words of Jane Goodall, the eminent biologist: '*Christine Stevens was a giant voice for animal welfare. Passionate, yet always reasoned, she took up one cause after another and she never gave up. Millions of animals are better off because of Christine's quiet and very effective advocacy.*'

Mother Teresa

The greatest humanitarian and the most inspirational lady of my lifetime was Mother Teresa, whom I met on my third visit to India in 1984. My sister Claire and her daughter had spent six months doing voluntary work at Mother Teresa's hospital in Calcutta and they asked me to take medical supplies and other gifts to help the work of the hospital. Mother Teresa was regarded as an icon by my sisters and we had all supported her cause for several years, so I was now keen to visit one of her centres. Born in Macedonia of Albanian descent, Mother Teresa left her homeland at the age of eighteen to become a Catholic missionary. She joined the Sisters of Loreto, an Irish group that had missions in India and first had to train in Ireland and learn English, as this was the teaching language used by the Sisters of Loreto in India.

In 1929 she was sent to India as a teacher and taught at St Mary's High School from 1931 until 1948 when she was finally allowed to leave the convent school, as she wanted to devote the rest of her life to working in the slum areas amongst the poorest people. Eventually

1981. Visiting Mother Teresa's Centre in Bombay, India.

Credit: RdeT collection

in 1950 she was given permission by the Vatican to start her own mission which later became known as 'Missionaries of Charity', with the main aim being (in her own words): *'to care for the hungry, the naked, the homeless, the crippled, the blind, the lepers, all those who feel unwanted, unloved, uncared for throughout society, people who have become a burden to society and are shunned by everyone.'*

Her first centre was opened in Calcutta and now almost sixty years later the charity has centres in more than 130 countries.

On this visit to India I was the guest of Mr and Mrs Boga, Indian business people living in Bombay, now called Mumbai. My hosts were delightful and so accommodating, arranging for me to visit other cities in India, knowing that I wanted to make the most of every minute and see as much as possible of this mystical country. However they were somewhat bemused when I asked for my itinerary to include slum areas in each city we would be visiting.

1981. Bombay, India. Visiting a centre for disabled people (back row, 4th from left).

Credit: RdeT collection

I hastily assured them that while I appreciated the splendour and comfort of their lifestyle, through travelling to many countries in the world, I had developed a great interest in social issues – human and animal welfare – and I wanted to understand as much as I could about the situation in India. They probably found me to be a rather unusual house guest.

As I had already seen considerable evidence of human and animal deprivation on the streets of India during my previous two visits: beggars; street children; wild animals; semi-feral animals; draught animals, all in need of care and compassion, I was intrigued to find out if the extremes in affluence and poverty were typical of other cities in India.

My hosts arranged for me to visit Pune and Hyderabad so I was able to visit all the main tourist areas in those cities, admire the architecture, and enjoy the beauty and charm of the Indian people.

196

In contrast I was also able to see the undeniable squalor and humiliation of life in the slum areas.

Mrs Boga arranged for me to visit the Mother Teresa Centre in Bombay (Mumbai) and much to my delight Mother Teresa was staying there and would be able to show me around the hospital. I was so excited and overwhelmed when this tiny, determined, compassionate Catholic lady met me at the gate and greeted me; her piercing eyes seemed to penetrate into my soul. I felt so in awe, yet humbled as she took me around the hospital explaining how and why they ran the centre.

She took me on a tour of the wards which were immaculate, the beds positioned in long rows opposite each other, the smooth bed covers looking fresh and neat. Each bed was occupied by a sick person; many had terminal illnesses. Patients waved a welcome to us as we walked around and Mother Teresa explained that she never turned anyone away and that she and her Sisters actively sought out those who were desperate, diseased and dying. They would bring such individuals into the hospital and give them a wash, clean clothes, a clean bed and offer a tray of different types of food. After being cleaned and fed, the patient would usually go to sleep knowing that at last they were free from the trauma and dangers of living on the streets. Some of the elderly and diseased died within a few days, but at least they were able to die with some element of dignity in the loving care of those devoted to relieving human suffering.

She told me of the day a businessman contacted her centre and told the nuns of a man he had seen every day for a week, huddled against a wall, who was obviously in need of help. The ambulance went to his aid and looking up with misty eyes, he simply said: '*I was waiting for you to come for me.*' He was taken to the centre where he was washed, given clean clothes, a clean bed and offered some food ... he died that night.

This course of action struck a chord with me and in my quiet moments I recalled Mother Teresa describing the main aims of her work: '*to care for the hungry, the naked, the homeless, the crippled, the blind, the lepers, all those who feel unwanted, unloved, uncared for throughout society, people who have become a burden to society and are shunned by everyone.*'

I realised that at *Refuge de Thiernay* we were also trying to apply these basic principles for animals, by accepting any animal in need, especially the old and terminally sick animals which in reality have little, if any future. Since we started the Refuge and to this day, we aim to give each animal at least a few days of comfort and care before their final day arrives, whether the animal dies from natural causes or is euthanised for a specific, inevitable reason.

When my visit to the centre finished, the Sisters waved farewell, singing a song for my safe journey back to France that day; somehow I couldn't tell them that I was not returning to France, but was on my way to Pune.

I learned some important lessons through my visits to India; I learned what compassion really means and that without action, compassion is meaningless. I learned that Mother Teresa truly cared for people and could see beauty in the ugliest situation.

I do not intend to imply that the work of *Refuge de Thiernay* is comparable to the extensive worldwide activity of Mother Teresa's centres, or that I or any of my staff mirror Mother Teresa – a Nobel Peace Prize recipient! Indeed there are those who regard me and my staff as eccentric 'do-gooders' who prefer animals to people (not true, we feel they are equally valuable). There are also those who label us as 'killers' for admitting that sometimes euthanasia is a considered action we sadly have to take. However those of us who work at *Refuge de Thiernay* do try to regard every animal as a valued being, try to see beauty in the difficult days and try to extend compassion with action. In the words of Mother Teresa we aim to care for those animals who are: '*hungry, the homeless, the crippled, the blind, all those unwanted, unloved, uncared for throughout society who have become a burden to society and are shunned.*'

11

Yesterday, Today and Beyond

Many suggestions were put forward by friends for the title of this book and when the word 'Panchiao' was suggested it was almost chosen, as it was one of the most meaningful words in my life. It was the name I gave to the little dog I chose to take home from the Pan Chiao government dog pound in Taiwan, the dog I call 'the love of my life'. But why did I choose him out of the several hundred dogs crammed together in the outdoor enclosures? I simply don't know, but feel it must have been through destiny rather than deliberate choice.

It was 1997 and I was with Wu Hung, Yu Min, Asa and Joy looking round the dog pound where volunteers were busy cleaning the kennels. Although the pound was far from ideal, it was a vast improvement on the previous Pan Chiao pound which had been exposed by Wu Hung and LCA some two years before, resulting in media attention from many parts of the world.

When the government of Taiwan finally accepted that it was inhumane to treat companion animals in this appalling way, they started to build new facilities and allocated a budget for the management of stray animals.

The original pound was just a few enclosures made of rusting wires and rotting wood, where dogs regardless of age, shape, or size, were packed tightly together and left to die; either through disease, injury or starvation. The dogs had been either collected by the dog catchers from the streets, or given up by their owners.

By marked contrast, the new Pan Chiao dog pound had many enclosures, with the sides and dividing panels constructed from galvanised steel, all having concrete bases. At the previous pound there were no designated staff or any veterinary attention, but the new Pan Chiao pound had a manager, staff, a veterinarian and several volunteers to clean the kennels. So while this was indeed a huge step forward, it was clear that the staff and volunteers needed help understanding the needs of the animals. Large dogs such as Japanese akitas and samoyeds acting aggressively, were in the same kennels as small dogs such as chihuahuas and pomeranians who were terrified of their kennel mates' behaviour, while a labrador crossbred type, was trying to mount an unwilling spaniel. Although a bowl of food and a bowl of water were in each kennel, only the dominant dogs would be able to eat and drink from them.

As we walked along the row of kennels, almost simultaneously Joy and I spied this tiny ball of orange fur cowering against the dividing panel of the kennel, trying to make himself invisible. Joy looked at me and said: '*You should take this dog.*'

I hadn't even thought about taking a dog back to France on this visit, but as soon as I saw him, I knew he was mine.

1997. The day I found Panchiao, the 'love of my life' at the Pan Chiao dog pound in Taiwan.

Credit: WSPA/LCA

The volunteer removed the terrified bundle from the kennel and put him into my arms. What a pathetic little dog! He was quite old, had a broken leg, was blind in one eye and I could feel through his matted fur that he was very thin.

The media in Taipei soon learned that I had chosen a dog from the Pan Chiao dog pound and one journalist asked me in a very serious voice: '*Will this dog be a prince in France?*' I replied in an equally serious voice: '*Yes, he will be the prince of my heart!*'

Once home in France, Panchiao seemed to know instantly what was expected of him and he found a new lease of life, no longer looking old and scared. He was such an accommodating little dog, never showing aggression or jealousy towards the other dogs and cats that share my home. It was as if he had been there before and the look in his one eye seemed to convey to me, *I trust you.* He was my constant companion for just four years and then one day he became ill and died from the human equivalent of a stroke, but through that little dog's life my contacts and interest in Asian countries continued to grow.

He was a great favourite with readers of my Refuge magazine, as his story aroused great curiosity. After all, it was unusual to hear about a dog being rescued from Taiwan, the Republic of China and taken to a backwater in France. In one of my more sentimental moments I wrote this story for younger readers:

Story of Panchiao: 9 July 1997

Once in a far away country called Taiwan, there was a sad little brown pomeranian with a broken leg and only one eye; it was little me.

My early memories are unclear, all I can recall is wandering around the streets of Taipei feeling hungry and not really knowing where to go, when suddenly two men ran at me with loops of wire in their hands. I tried to run away from them but my little legs would not respond quickly enough. Suddenly I screamed; intense pain engulfed my tiny body as a catching wire was thrown over my head and pulled tightly.

201

I was thrown into a large cage on the back of the waiting vehicle where there were already several large dogs, all with wires embedded in their necks. Some were screaming in agony, others frozen through pain and fear, and I was petrified. I crawled into a corner of the vehicle and hid my head trying to keep still, as the wire around my neck was causing me so much pain. I think I must have fainted as my next memory is being dragged out of the vehicle and thrown into an enclosure with hundreds of dogs of all shapes and sizes. Had I died and gone to another world? Not exactly, I was at the Pan Chiao government dog pound.

I stayed as still as I could for days and days, not daring to look around me as the whining and groaning of other dogs filled me with fear.

Then one day I saw several people staring at me and I heard the sound of voices uttering strange noises which sounded like joy, wspa, wu hung, lca, yumin – what did these sounds mean? I was desperately trying to hide as I felt sure the noises meant that something even worse was going to happen to me. Then to my horror I was picked up and after a few moments of terror I was placed into the arms of an unusual creature the other people called Princess who immediately began whispering to me.

What was going on? She didn't seem angry with me; she held me gently and removed the wire from around my neck. A tear dropped from her eye as she told me she loved me – was she mad? I gathered from the Chinese people around her that she had spotted me amongst the other 400 dogs looking so forlorn and full of despair. She had fallen in love with me instantly and wanted to take me to another country, to her home in France. Suddenly men were taking photographs of me with the princess and through an interpreter I was told that I was never going to be imprisoned again, but was to become a prince. Now I felt sure that all the trauma of the past few weeks must have destroyed my brain, or perhaps the whole world really had gone mad. I felt absolutely terrified and my tiny body trembled.

However I was so wrong and later I was put in a comfortable box having been bathed and groomed, with my injuries treated, then my box was put into what I thought was an enormous dog pound van which leapt into the sky and roared for more than 20 hours. The next words I heard were Charles de Gaulle Aérogare – I was in France – once again I was terrified!

I was taken to a place where a man in green clothes called Dr Dubreuil looked in my mouth, examined my skin, and frowned at my broken leg and what had happened to my eye. My broken leg and blind eye were war wounds from battles in the dog pound. I was fortunate to still be alive, although at the time it happened I just wanted to die.

Within a few hours I arrived at a paradise called home where I was greeted royally by the princess and her helpers. Everyone smiled and cooed at me making strange noises in French. Was I dreaming? No everyone seemed happy and although they looked strange to me, with features and a language quite different to Chinese people, they didn't seem mad! I was given a beautiful collar embossed with coloured stones with a medallion hanging from it with my new name inscribed Panchiao, named after the town where I was chosen by the princess. The name means wooden bridge and I was to become the bridge, the link, between the animal welfare campaigners in France and Taiwan.

My time is now spent bouncing around with the dogs and the horses, then I bounce home again and sit on the toes of Princess while she speaks on the phone to joy, wspa, wu hung, lca, yumin – I now know that these words played a large part in my new wonderful life with Princess.

At night I have my own tartan blanket on which to sleep and in my dreams I hear those magic words again and again ... Every day the princess tells me that she loves me and that I will never be unhappy again as I am the prince of her heart.

Little Prince Panchiao

P.S. Not only am I now a prince, but I have been promoted to an ambassador for non-stop letter-writing as I represent all the Taiwan government pound dogs, and I am now brave enough to bark ferociously at the government officials, just like the princess and the staff here at Refuge de Thiernay.

On Reflection

I think my motivation for setting up an animal shelter was in my genes and I was born programmed to follow the road to the Refuge. Aunt Marie was also very close to nature and animals, likewise other ancestors and my sisters. My cousin told me that in the nineteenth century when her great-grandmother died, she left her château to her cat – there was a lawsuit and the cat lost! Her daughter rescued working horses from the mines and had a gift for taming foxes and wild birds. She wore a badge pinned to her fur coat, inscribed with the words 'humanitarian fur' but I'm not sure what that term meant in those days.

Although I am the only person in my family who until recently has followed animal welfare as a career, to my great delight my niece, Léopoldine, the daughter of my sister Mella, now works in animal welfare administration. Léopoldine has recently married and lives at Mânoir de Valotte, the former home of my late sister Mimi, which has been in our family for centuries.

My sisters, their children and now their grandchildren, have a strong awareness of animal welfare which is largely due to the influence of our English nannies appointed to take care of me and my siblings, which we have passed on to the younger generations. Our nannies taught us to be aware of the beauty of nature, animals and humans. In particular, one of our nurses, Elisabeth Ranby, who was very strict, taught us to listen to the birds and find peace and simple pleasure growing vegetables in our kitchen garden. Also she taught us to be kind to each other.

Activities in France

In France I am a Vice-President of the *Conseil National de La Protection Animale* (*CNPA*) which is an association set up by veterinarian Dr Fernand Méry in 1970 under the patronage of the Ministry of Agriculture. Dr Jean-Pierre Kieffer, a veterinarian friend in Paris, is the *Secrétaire Général*.

CNPA functions as a think tank and the board of administration

2008. With Dr Jean-Pierre Kieffer, President of l'OABA at his office in Paris.

Credit: JLL

is made up mainly of veterinarians, a lawyer, a journalist and other professionals, who also serve on various advisory committees. Dr Méry invited me to join the board for public relations purposes, soon after *CNPA* was set up.

CNPA which is a founding member of Eurogroup for Animal Welfare, has the ear of central government and is the official spokesperson for animal protection in France, so it is in a strong position to advise and comment on any proposed change to the law. Some of the issues which *CNPA* has been working on in recent years have all met with some measure of success. These include the transport of animals; veal crates; battery hens; sow stalls; ritual slaughter; pet identification and education of pet owners. We are fortunate to have such an organisation in France and although animal welfare workers in the field may sometimes question what *CNPA* does as there is no direct hands-on animal activity, I can assure you that the scientific, educational and legal expertise amongst the board is invaluable for the future protection of animals in France.

Receiving the Chevalier de l'Ordre National du Mérite awarded by the President of the French Republic in 1979.

Credit: CNPA

I have been honoured to receive several awards for my work with animals, including:

1979: *Chevalier de l'Ordre National du Mérite*, awarded by the President of the French Republic: for work with *Conseil National de la Protection Animale.*

1984: *Diplôme d'Honneur* awarded by *La Ligue Française pour la Protection du Cheval*: for services to rescue horses.

1994: The American Society for the Prevention of Cruelty to Animals Founders Award: for lifelong dedication to the promotion of kindness and compassion towards animals.

2005: The St Stephen's Medal awarded by the Minister of Culture, Ukraine: for assisting in the humane management of stray animals in Kiev.

2006: The Humane Society of the United States/Humane Society International Award for Extraordinary Commitment and Achievement.

2006. Dr Andrew Rowan presenting the HSU/HSI Award for Extraordinary Commitment and Achievement.

Credit: HSUS

Patron of Small Societies

I have more than enough animals to care for in my own Refuge, but I closely follow the work of other animal charities and try to give support where I can. However, although I have often been asked, I rarely agree to become a trustee or patron of any charity. Greyhounds in Nood Belgium (GINB) is one exception and I am official godmother to the dogs!

Why did I agree to be a patron? Well, as I am Belgian I am pleased to support a Belgian society, especially the admirable work of GINB, an organisation set up by Mireille Broeders in 1996 to save abused and abandoned greyhounds and galgos from a torturous death in Spain. Greyhounds race at dog tracks, while galgos, a Spanish breed of dog similar to a small greyhound, are trained to hunt rabbits and boars.

Historically, galgos used for hunting during the good weather, were

2000 Spain. Examining a galgo which was found hanging from a tree.

Credit: GNIB

2001. At a conference with veterinary students in Manila.

Credit: HSUS

2006 HSUS EXPO Dallas. Having fun with friends after the conference.
Left to right: Ken Grant, Sherry Grant, Neil Trent, Jack Reece, me,
Victoria Kizinievic, Yuli Weston.

Credit: HSUS

disposed of before winter set in. If the dog failed to impress his
owner or performed badly, he could be disposed of by a cruel method
such as hanging, drowning, being burned alive or even worse.
Fortunately, in recent years, through continuous lobbying by GINB
and other groups in Europe, the situation has been improving slowly.
An animal protection law was passed in Spain in 2003 which states
that anyone found guilty of causing death or injury to an animal
will be sent to prison for a period of up to a year. However it is
unusual for anyone to be prosecuted as the law is rarely enforced.

In recent years, fewer animals are hanged, but more are abandoned
– often with their legs broken to prevent them finding their way
home. GINB rescues as many as possible, transports the dogs from
Spain to Belgium in a specially equipped air-conditioned truck and
finds the right type of family in Belgium for each dog.

I first met Mireille about twelve years ago when she came to the
Refuge de Thiernay to collect some greyhounds that had been rescued

from the racing tracks in Spain. Another charity had brought them to me and Mireille had found them suitable homes in Belgium. Mireille had just started her own organisation and I agreed to go to her first fund-raising event, the election of Miss and Mr GINB! It was perfectly organised with media coverage and lots of interest from the public.

I have been to Spain with GINB and seen at first hand their work and have now attended several of their fund-raising events in Belgium. I am impressed with their achievements in such a short time-span; the creation of their information centre; the specifically equipped transport vehicle; the public education materials – all done so professionally. They are an excellent example of how a small society can make a big difference. Never underestimate the strength and influence of the individual, or the small societies.

I am also a patron of two other small societies, SNIP International and ARC, both based in the UK. SNIP International was set up in 1996 as an offshoot of SNIP UK, the brainchild of Kate Horne and as the name suggests, promotes neutering programmes for stray and feral animals, mainly cats. SNIP International, now a separate organisation, is coordinated by Linda Brookes from her home in Cornwall and works globally providing humane equipment for practical projects and expertise through volunteer veterinarians.

Animal Rescue Charity (ARC) is an animal rescue centre in Bishop's Stortford, Hertfordshire, set up by Jan Rose and Fiona Piggott in 1990 and managed by Cherry Mitchell, to provide a safe haven for neglected, unwanted and abandoned animals and wherever possible, to treat and rehabilitate all animals, including wildlife. Again, two small societies doing good work and I am pleased to support their efforts.

If I could start again what would I do differently? Well, if I had been wealthy then certainly the facilities at the *Refuge de Thiernay* would have been built and maintained to a higher standard and the financial headaches over the years would have been non-existent. But I have no regrets devoting my time and energy to animal welfare, as I still believe that it is a most important job. Over the past forty years my animal welfare friends have become my family and we share common thinking on the health and welfare of all species. If I could start again I would give higher priority to education, my own education and animal welfare education for the general public. When I started my Refuge I was so busy trying to cope with caring for the animals, I had no time to develop education programmes. Over the years we did develop some educational activities, but on an 'ad hoc' basis, when time and manpower allowed, now I realise that education should have been an integral part of my work from the beginning.

I have always hated injustice of any kind through racism, bullying, poverty, greed and malice. This has led me to question over and over again why many governments seem oblivious to poverty in their countries – poverty which continues for centuries, even though there is extreme affluence for a privileged few. Surely a concerted effort to end poverty should be a priority, but corruption seems totally to ignore the plight of others. In 2001 I was in Manila for an animal welfare conference organised by the Philippine Animal Welfare Society and sponsored by HSUS/HSI, IFAW and the Hong Kong SPCA. I was staying in a most comfortable hotel through the generosity of these sponsors, and each morning I filled my pockets with as much food as I could carry from the buffet breakfast table and gave it to the hungry street children who collected outside the hotels.

I clearly remember a thin ragged little boy of about eight, a regular, who would snatch whatever I offered and run away. I can still imagine him waiting for me on the day after I left the hotel when I failed to turn up with food for him. I know that other people who stayed at the hotel may have given him food, so it is unlikely he would have starved, but how unjust it seems in this modern world for a little boy to have to depend on crumbs from the table of others.

My journey through life has taken a long, winding road with many potholes along the way and now in the twilight of my life I feel twinges of sadness that I cannot do more. Since the dawn of man centuries ago, many millions of animals have been used for man's pleasure, for food, for work, often used and abused through ignorance and indifference. But in my lifetime thankfully I have seen some positive changes, such as an improvement in treatment and attitudes towards animals in circuses, farm animals and companion animals. Also there is a general acceptance that animals experience emotions and sensations, including pain and can therefore suffer. There are many more animal welfare groups around the world than when I started and the veterinary profession has come much closer to us. Here in France there is definitely an awakening awareness of animals and their needs, although by UK standards of animal welfare, we still have a long way to go before we catch up. As for the future of mankind, sometimes the battle seems to be never-ending with wars between countries and civil wars taking place around the world more than at any time in history, so the charities set up to provide relief from human suffering and poverty are needed more than ever.

But many situations **have** changed which will mean better lives for future generations: for many years there was an apartheid system in the USA and South Africa; there was a wall dividing Western and Eastern Europe; there was enforced communism in many countries, but now this has all changed, bringing opportunities for many people of the world. No doubt we can all give examples of some lives that are now worse off than in the past, but speaking from experience, although life is uncertain, it can indeed be rewarding and fulfilling, as long as we use our hearts and our minds to *do something useful* for our fellow human beings and all other living beings.

12

In Conclusion

The Relaxation Letters

How do I relax? With difficulty, as there is always so much to do, but I do try!

Audrey Burns Ross is a lovely friend who does humanitarian work with a quiet selfless approach. She is a holistic yoga and relaxation teacher and the author of two books. I first met her in 1993 when she invited me to contribute to a book she was compiling, called *The Relaxation Letters*. Later that year I went to a successful high-profile auction at Sotheby's in London, held to raise funds for United Nations Children's Fund (UNICEF), of which Audrey was the chairperson of the organising committee.

I agreed to contribute to *The Relaxation Letters*, along with 136 other contributors, including the Dalai Lama; the Archbishop of Canterbury; Mother Teresa; Bob Geldof; the Hon Benazir Bhutto and Billy Graham. The royalties from this inspirational book were donated to UNICEF and Friends of the Earth.

To help the contributors focus their thinking, Audrey posed three questions to us:

- How do you relax and unwind?
- What is your general philosophy of life?
- Do you have a poem, passage or any words that have given you inspiration in life?

My following letter, as published in *The Relaxation Letters*, attempts to answer these questions:

213

My work is my relaxation, although I do find time occasionally to play a game of patience.

My philosophy of life is very much rooted in the philosophy of my parents who believed that, if one is given great privilege, one must, in turn, help others. They did this in a discreet way, and now, as I grow older, I realize what a tremendous impression they made on me.

I believe we should devote time in our lives to other people, other creatures. We owe it to them. After encountering great tragedies in the world I became very aware of suffering, human and animal. This prompted me to do more. Consequently I now devote my life to my work, and never really know what is going to happen next. I am involved seven days a week for fifty-two weeks of the year.

I am spiritually recharged by my work and it makes me feel very happy to be able to help. I live in perpetual enchantment and look at an animal as I would a work of art. The same applies when I see the frightened face of a child who has suffered break into a smile.

I believe relaxation and peace of mind can be achieved by doing something one really believes in.

*In the end, we have all to account for what we have done, and, while we are here on this earth, there is so much injustice to be tackled. My great feeling is that we must share what we have and help in every possible way we can by physically **DOING SOMETHING**.*

Love and Thanks

I could not write this book without thanking many people who have helped me so willingly along the way and who continue to support my charity. I have been so fortunate to have volunteer help and advice from my English friends over the years, such as David and Tim Barnes, Peter and Linda Brookes, Richard and Elizabeth Daymond, Ed and Isobelle Egan, Graham and Moya Fuller, David Griffiths and Linda, Bill and Mary Hames, Stacey Irwin, Caroline Yates and Joy Lee from the Mayhew, David and Cherry Mitchell and John, James and Jackie Thorburn. Some of them have transformed the facilities

13 December 2001. Friends arrived unexpectedly for my 80th birthday, having arranged a surprise party for me at a restaurant in Nevers. It was a wonderful day and I was amazed when Wu Hung appeared from under the table as I had no idea he was in Europe!

Credit: RdeT collection

with maintenance work such as painting, fencing and kennel repairs, others have helped with practical work caring for the animals at the Refuge and with administration, while others have never been too busy to listen to my concerns and offer me sound advice. I also owe so much to Pierre Quartier, a faithful volunteer who was with me during those tough early days at the Refuge, when we had little more than grit determination and raw enthusiasm.

In addition to this help, many professional kennel staff sent annually by Clarissa Baldwin, Chief Executive Officer of Dogs Trust, have given us wonderful support for the past 10 years. Dennis Baker, Chief Executive Officer of WGAS has also sent staff to help us and has found adoptive families in the UK for some of our Refuge dogs.

We are fortunate to have help with re-homing animals, from friends and animal welfare societies in neighbouring countries: Lilian and Gertjan Bolkensteijn in the Netherlands; *Tierheim Pforzheim* in Germany

215

1997. At *Refuge de Thiernay* with some of my staff: Odile Clément with Jaunet, me with Fu-lee and Nadège Darneau with Panchiao.

Credit: RdeT collection

and *Société Genevoise pour la Protection des Animaux*, Switzerland. They come to our aid from time to time without fail and do what we struggle to do in France – find good homes for all the unwanted animals that are brought to us.

Other wonderful friends are John Ruane and Caroline Barker of Naturewatch, who besides giving me the opportunity to work with them in Ukraine, indeed did us a great favour when they recommended Victoria Kizinievic to us, a veterinary student from Lithuania who wanted to get experience doing practical work at an animal shelter.

She came to *Refuge de Thiernay* for four consecutive years during her summer holidays and worked as a residential volunteer. She was absolutely lovely, talented and hard working and assisted Dr Griffiths with the neutering programme and other surgical procedures. Victoria, a member of the Lithuanian SPCA, is now a qualified veterinarian.

For more than thirty years, I had a wonderful working relationship with WSPA staff who always found time to help and advise; dedicated people such as John Callaghan, David Street, Ali Findlay, Brian

2000. Marie-Christine Thelliez, Administrator at *Refuge de Thiernay.*

Credit: RdeT collection

Faulkner, Dragan Nastic, Jonathan Pearce, Jonathan Owen, Claire Palmer, 'the clean girls' Dawn Peacock and Charlotte Scott, Victor Watkins, Phil Wilson and Trevor Wheeler – a great joker, a lovely man who can always make me laugh. I think of them all as my extended family.

Everyone mentioned (and others who know who they are but prefer to remain anonymous), have boosted my morale with their enthusiasm and encouragement, especially at times when I have been despondent faced with an overcrowded shelter and worried about paying the bills.

My French friends, trustees and supporters have played such a large part over the years, encouraging me with humanitarian and animal-related activities and helping me with mundane, but important, jobs such as sorting out clothes and donated goods for Romania, Poland, Ukraine and Mother Teresa's centres. My long-serving staff have never failed to support me: Odile Clément, Nadège Darneau, Marie-Christine Thelliez, Aurélien Derouvois, Mary de Jong and long-term volunteers Josiane Cœuret, Marie-France Derouvois, Liesbeth Kortbeek, Héliande Dru, also my nephew Charles who is a neighbouring farmer and brings the hay and straw for the horses and farm animals living at the Refuge.

217

2008. Nico Joiner, Canine Carer at Canterbury Dogs Trust Rehoming Centre. Nico came to help us at *Refuge de Thiernay* and adopted 'Cooper' a sad, thin dog who was brought into the Refuge after years of neglect. Nico and Cooper now live happily together in the UK

Credit: RdeT collection

All continue to give so much support and commitment to our work. My great friend, Nicole Delsaux, always lends a sympathetic ear when I am low in spirits, as we have been friends for more than sixty years. Nicole is a trustee of my charity and has a calming influence on me when I am stressed and agitated. For more than thirty-five years she has worked at the Louvre in Paris and is a specialist on the restoration of icons, having restored more than 100 in the past five years.

At times, problems at the Refuge such as the constant influx of cruelty cases, animals stolen, abusive owners and general work overload, seems to be never-ending. However, when one feels despondent, often the clouds start to lift and better days emerge as wonderful adopters turn up and choose the most sad little dog, the ugliest cat, or the animal that has been at the Refuge the longest, and one's faith in human nature is restored. All of you who work in animal shelters will know exactly what I mean.

2009. With my great, great nephews and niece, Manuela, Tiago, and Alexis who all love animals.

Credit: RdeT collection

A good example in recent years is the story of Roby, an old black and white cross-bred fox terrier who was terrified and in a traumatised state when he was found abandoned and brought to us still attached to a heavy chain, which weighed more than 2.5 kg. His owner was known, but we refused to return Roby to this callous man. After a long period of careful nursing, we arranged for Roby to be sent to the UK and rehomed through Wood Green Animal Shelters. Roby was in luck. He was adopted by Jeannie and Colin Davidson and was able to enjoy the most wonderful loving home for just a short period before he died. But the story does not end there. His adoptive family were so inspired by this brave and responsive little dog that they now do voluntary work at WGAS and help other animals to regain their trust in humans. And last year Jeannie and her friend Bibiane Bedford, also a volunteer at WGAS, came to help us at *Refuge de Thiernay*. Thank you Roby for giving us humans another chance.

There are so many other people who work in animal welfare in far more difficult circumstances than I have ever encountered: people in developing countries; those suffering from the devastation of civil war. People such as Dr Jalloh, helping stray animals in Sierra Leone where rabies is endemic; a country with widespread poverty trying to recover from eight years of civil war and Rosemary Gordon pioneering spay and neuter programmes in the desert areas of Peru and Nora Garcia who has ploughed on for years, working her way through the red tape of Cuba and getting back up when knocked down. So many other individuals work with little recognition. I understand some of their difficulties and pay tribute to what they do to help animals as they are extending the worldwide animal welfare family. As often quoted: 'animal welfare is indeed an extension of humanity'.

Sherry Grant and Dr Listriani from the organisation *Yudisthira* in Bali, Indonesia have set up some wonderful education classes to go alongside their animal treatment and neutering programmes. I visited Bali in 2001 and went to a field clinic near the village of Tanalot. There were about fifty children, aged about eight to ten, all eagerly learning about the care and treatment of animals. Then I watched in a school classroom as children were taught about their native animals through the use of finger puppets. I had harboured thoughts and dreams of an education centre at *Refuge de Thiernay* for some time and while watching these children I knew that I must make this dream a reality.

Finally, to all of you who have helped me and inspired me in so many different ways, you will never know just how much your kindness and warm friendship has meant to me. I have been truly blessed – my love and thanks to you all.

Elizabeth de Croÿ

Elisabeth in Action, as Told by Others

With Elisabeth in Poland: as told by Jenny Remfry

My first meeting with the charismatic Princess Elisabeth de Croÿ was unforgettable. It happened like this: in January 1989 I was instructed by the Director of WSPA to go to Poland to make contact with the animal protection societies. I protested that although I was the Regional Director for Europe I had never been to Poland and would not know where to start. I was then informed that I would accompany Elisabeth, who had all the right contacts, and that I would be introduced to her at a Eurogroup meeting in Paris. So I went to the meeting, and this elegant, aristocratic lady came up to me and said in her deep voice in English only slightly accented by French, '*You must be Dr Remfry, let us go to Poland together. We need to help the poor people and animals of that sad, hungry country.*'

I said that I would be delighted, but would there not be problems about travelling in the communist bloc?

'*You are not to worry. We will take plenty of American dollars, in 1 dollar bills, well hidden in our body belts, and packets of cigarettes, and we will get through.*'

I asked whether there were suitable hotels for us to stay in.

'*I never stay in hotels. We will go to the monasteries.*'

I suggested that convents would be more appropriate.

'*Oh no, one is always far better received by the monks.*'

Bemused, I returned to London and awaited developments. They came in March.

'*Jenny, the people of France have been so generous with their donations*

223

of food, household materials and medicines that it will not all fit into my car.'

I asked what the solution to that problem may be.

'We must hire a lorry. But Jenny, would it be fitting for two ladies to drive a lorry across Europe? Should we not take a driver with us?'

'OK, who do you suggest?'

'I have met a young Polish pianist in Paris, who longs to return to his native land. He is so charming and so sensitive. He would like to drive us. But there is another possibility. Mr Adam is a good driver and is willing to come.'

'Who is Mr Adam?' I enquired.

'He is my plumber.'

'Well, I think a plumber could be more useful than a pianist.'

'I agree absolutely. We will go in April.'

So we met in Strasbourg and I loaded some cat and dog catching equipment into the large hired van. Early next morning we set off across France and Germany to the Czech border. There, with the help of Elisabeth's passport, which read something like *The King of the Belgians requests free passage to his beloved cousin, Her Serene Highness the Princess Elisabeth de Croÿ-Solre* and a packet of cigarettes, we entered and reached Prague. Next day we entered Poland and arrived in Wroclaw. There we met Elisabeth's most useful contact, an entomologist from the University of Krakow called Professor Anna Czapik. So now we were a princess, a plumber, a professor and me, and we could not all fit in the cab of the van.

We took it in turns to sit inside the van, in darkness, sitting on a pile of clothes, and it so happened that it was Elisabeth's turn inside when we arrived at Krakow, where the press had gathered to meet and interview her. They watched in amazement as she descended from the bowels of the van and immediately began to tell them about our mission of mercy.

The monastery in Wroclaw was hospitable, but not nearly as grand as the monastery attached to the cathedral in Krakow. Elisabeth always presented herself well, but for the guestmaster in Krakow she took extra care: hair groomed; jewellery selected; nails varnished, and plenty of perfume. The monks were mesmerised and listened in rapt attention as she led the conversation at table. Food was short, and we ate mostly soup and bread with a bit of cheese and ham; I remember being quite excited one day when I saw a crate of carrots being brought in. We gave the food, clothes, household materials and medicines to the monks to distribute, and took the animal food and medicines and the catching equipment to the animal shelters.

The power of Elisabeth's charisma was perhaps best demonstrated at Austerlitz. On our way back from Krakow to Prague, our driver Adam wanted particularly to visit the museum at the battlefield made famous by Napoleon Bonaparte. We arrived at dusk, just as two men were locking the gates for the night. Elisabeth begged them to let us in, explaining that we had come such a long way; that we would never be able to come this way again; that it was Adam's lifelong ambition to visit the museum, housed in the castle occupied by his great hero Napoleon after the battle. The men were the director and the electrician of the museum.

How could they refuse? They let us in, gave us a conducted tour, opened up the attic to show us the boxes of uniform buttons, horseshoes, weapons etc collected from the site, and the tin soldiers manufactured as souvenirs of the battle. They did not know who we were, because we did not introduce ourselves, but they made us coffee, opened a bottle of wine, and finally invited us to sign the VIP visitors' book. Elisabeth wrote her name under the signature of Henry Kissinger!

Refuge de Thiernay Investigations: as told by Josiane Cœuret

How did I become an animal investigator for *Refuge de Thiernay*? My first contact with the Refuge was in connection with a neighbour's dog that was locked up in a flat and rarely taken out, the owner coming home drunk every night. Like many people, I really liked animals but had no idea how many were abused, as naively I thought that if anyone took on a dog, they would obviously care for it. After Princess negotiated with the owner, he surrendered the dog to the Refuge and it was found a loving home.

Princess asked me if I could volunteer some time to help her with letter writing and other administrative duties, as she was overwhelmed with paperwork. I agreed. Shortly after this, she asked me to meet her at 9 p.m. in a village close to where I lived, as she had been called to rescue a German shepherd dog with its leg caught in a leg-hold trap. A local man had set the trap to catch a fox as his rabbits were regularly being killed and eaten, but instead of catching a fox, a dog had been trapped.

Although setting a trap is relatively easy, releasing a struggling dog can be difficult and dangerous. Some men who were there kept a safe distance from the dog, but Princess, with great courage (or recklessness) opened the trap and quickly slipped a dog grasper over his head and held him firmly. I had never seen anyone do anything like this and I was full of admiration for her. Little did I realise at the time, but I was being groomed to investigate and rescue.

My next contact with Princess involved stealing chickens at night. An elderly vagrant had locked up a large dog in a cellar and didn't feed it, so with the help of a local forest guard and a policeman, we got it out through a small opening. However, three chickens and a rooster were left behind, amongst the carcasses of other dead birds. The authorities had no interest in the poultry and dismissed Princess's concerns for the birds, so having rescued the dog she did not argue further with the officials, but decided we would independently move the birds to the Refuge, late at night.

Catching a struggling, noisy bird during the middle of the night, without alerting neighbours, then putting it into a cat basket with its wings flapping angrily, is not an easy task. It was my baptism of fire in the ways of Princess. Since then I have travelled with a teammate around the Burgundy region, investigating situations where animals are unhappy and abused. Sometimes Princess comes too, disguised as a crazed-looking old woman in a scruffy coat and tattered headscarf.

To understand the challenges of animal protection in France, you need to first understand the cultural and traditional influences. France is not an Anglo-Saxon country, and the mentality is very different from the UK. It is a Latin country and although the treatment of animals historically is not as barbaric as Spain, Greece or Italy, it is closer to Latin countries than to north European ones. Although France has animal protection laws, they are seldom implemented and rarely is any real deterrent given to offenders. Traditionally in rural areas, there were just working dogs such as dogs to guard and herd the sheep, hounds used for hunting and guard dogs for business premises and family homes, whereas companion dogs tended to be owned by affluent people living in the towns and cities. But in recent years with the growth of consumerism in towns and rural areas, animals have become just another novelty that one gets rid of when the slightest problem arises.

Often, those who have the most animals are those who are least able to care for them, such as the underprivileged, social misfits and the mentally ill, and those without the financial means to care for an animal.

In order to deal with such situations, animal protection organisations use volunteer investigators, most of whom have the best intentions but little knowledge of the law or necessary animal handling skills. Such training does not exist in France, so the volunteer investigators do not always act wisely, and sometimes end up discrediting the animal protection cause.

In my case I learnt from Princess and developed my own philosophy, figuring that one cannot save all animals, that one does one's best, and destiny does the rest. At the beginning, one feels that one can save the world, but this thinking leads to sleepless nights and potential depression.

Investigations require time, patience, persuasion and careful monitoring. We document all reports and action and have to 'harass' the police to take the cases seriously. Cases I've been involved with include dogs that have been savagely beaten; dogs living on council housing balconies twenty-four hours a day; others in hot conservatories; in off-the-road cars; in dark cubbyholes; tied up to radiators and left without water; animals with ear infections, mange, infected eyes, hair glued together with excrement; animals abandoned, even cases of cats tied up on short tethers so they can only stay in their litter which is never cleaned; neglected equines with untrimmed hooves that take the shape of traditional Turkish slippers; sheep, cattle abandoned in barren pastures. The list is endless.

The following cases highlight some of the investigations we have made.

227

Case 1: A forest warden heard barking noises and saw two women leaving an isolated, unoccupied house. He contacted the Refuge giving the location of the house – perhaps an illegal breeder or stolen dogs?

When we eventually got into the house there were sixty-one dogs, including several puppies living in total darkness on piles of faeces. The owners of the dogs were a lady and her daughter, both of low intelligence, who hid the dogs at the house when their neighbours complained. There were no grounds for prosecution under French law, so the owners were allowed to keep nine of the dogs once the Refuge nursed them back to good health. However, they never came to collect them.

Case 2: We were told of a mentally handicapped couple, under guardianship, living on the outskirts of a small village, with six scrawny Labradors, several puppies and cats, all in dire need of care and food, so we called the veterinary services and the guardianship services. We all agreed that a policeman, a veterinarian, a social worker, and someone from the Refuge should visit the home and remove the animals.

The owners refused to allow any of the dogs to be taken away, screaming that the dogs were their babies. There were some chickens in the courtyard and the policeman, thinking he was calming the situation stupidly suggested that the chickens could be fed to the dogs, if the owners didn't have the money to feed them. The woman then became hysterical and fetched a knife which she brandished at the policeman screaming: '*You want to kill my babies.*' The situation was potentially dangerous for all of us so the visit was quickly abandoned that day.

However with patience and after several visits, we persuaded the couple to let the Refuge look after three of the dogs and neuter the three remaining bitches. This seemed to calm the situation, but ironically each time we visited, the couple would tell us about other people in the area who mistreated their animals.

Case 3: In January 2004 we were informed of animals that were badly looked after: puppies tied up under a shelter made of a metal sheet; two goats in a dark hut; a six-month-old foal in a flooded field, a cat, chickens and unfed rabbits. We spoke to the owners and asked if they would improve the living conditions for these animals, but before they did anything the cat and a dog were killed in road accidents and the rabbits, with one exception, had died.

In June the animals were moved to a field in the middle of the woods, without food or water and although we called the police station, and the veterinary services, there was no response from them, but we still kept filing reports.

In April the following year, the family moved to another location and kept a calf tied up in a concrete hut without food or water. Other animals, goats, pigs and chicken were also confined with no food or water. We contacted the police and veterinary services, but again we had no response.

Some two months later, the same calf, now a small cow, died in a field, tied up in the sun – the temperature was 35 degrees that day – with no water. The owners were away. We contacted the police yet again who called the slaughterman. Our complaint remains unanswered.

Just four months later the family moved yet again to another village and took their remaining animals with them. The foal, now a young horse was put in a field 25 kilometres away without water and we found her amongst old drums and rusted cans, barbed wire and two partly-decomposed goats. We called the veterinary services, but they refused to do anything, so we filed yet another complaint. The complaint was eventually transferred from the police to the court on 27 December 2005. We won the case and *Refuge de Thiernay* was given custody of the animals. The owner was given a small fine that he could not pay, but at least he was told he must never own an animal again.

As we waited for the case to be finalised, our investigator had to drive 50 kilometres a day to take water to the horse we named Pearl, as we were not allowed to have her at the Refuge while the trial was on. Finally, Pearl spent two years at the shelter until we found her a new home with responsible owners. So, although the owner was let off lightly, the eventual outcome for Pearl was well worth our persistent investigations.

With Naturewatch in Ukraine: as told by John Ruane

There was plenty of time before the flight back home. Still, I was tense. The check-in at Kyiv airport was always a lengthy affair. Hardly anyone spoke English and despite Ukraine's declaration of independence from Moscow, Soviet bureaucracy was alive and well, also we had a special guest travelling with us to Borispol Airport. She had an injured ankle wrapped in a large white bandage. We would need to be careful and take everything nice and slow as her leg was clearly painful and I was worried in case she might further injure herself on the car door, or slip on the uneven pavements.

This was the reason why I allowed over twice the normal time to get to the airport. Also on the way to the airport we would make a brief stop at an abandoned old building which used to be a hospital – it had now been taken over by an old Ukrainian lady who used it as an animal shelter.

We had heard bad reports about the conditions at the shelter but the old lady had the place well sealed up from any curious visitors. However, our driver knew when she would be away from the site and he knew how to gain access. Well, actually he had a key to the back door! He was very nervous and warned us that once at the shelter we must be extremely quick, we must get in and out of the building in the least possible time: take photos, give the animals some biscuits which we had in the car boot, and get out *fast*. If she came back and discovered what we were doing she would almost certainly lock us in as we were warned she was crazy!

So our plan was to get some photos of the conditions for the animals and then once back in UK we could contact the Ukrainian authorities and urge them to close the place. That was the plan: nice and simple, in and out fast, leave our guest with the bad ankle in the car – we would only be a few minutes. We arrived at the shelter. '*I want to come with you,*' said our guest. '*But your ankle,*' I protested.

'*Give me your arm and I will be fine. Oh and give me a bag of the food.*'

Against my better judgement, we made it in through the side door. God, it was a dark hallway and full of dogs; we couldn't see them, but we could feel them, then we saw the light and found ourselves in a filthy courtyard. I started to take photos and our guest started to feed the dogs. Soon the first bag was empty but we did have more. Another bag was opened. Beyond the courtyard we could see rooms where many dozens of dogs were barking. We moved over towards those rooms, there were lots of them. I guess old hospital wards and dogs everywhere. I had by now enough images to make a powerful case for the closure of this terrible place.

'*OK, let's go now – you ready?*' I urged. '*But there are more dogs and I want to feed them a few biscuits.*' she responded. '*OK, fine, but please hurry.*' Then I lost sight of her. Our driver became very agitated: '*If we don't leave now the old lady will be back soon and she will lock us in.*'

Our guest was still busy. She was pulling doors open to check if any animals were inside. Now I was really tense. '*Please, we really, really must leave now.*' Another ten minutes went by. Now our guest was 'double checking' she hadn't missed feeding any of the dogs. Then the hearing loss happened! What hearing loss? She hadn't mentioned any problems with her hearing. Our guest was in no rush and oblivious now to our pleas to get to the airport. She was feeding the animals and nothing was going to prevent her.

Yes, we did eventually get out and raced to the airport – no time for coffee or food – we had to rush our guest straight to the Air France flight. I remember the French plane officials complaining that our guest was the last one to board the plane and the captain was fearful of losing his departure slot. I just smiled at them and said: '*Welcome to the world of Princess Elisabeth de Croÿ where animals come first.*'

I turned to look at Princess who was beaming with delight. There was also a glint in her eyes. Yes, I got the message – animals first, everything else can wait.

There was no cruising speed. It was full throttle until we reached the necessary altitude and the captain turned off the seat belt lights. At last we were able to relax … but only until the next trip with Princess.

Over the coming years, I got to know that glint well … very well, which can be translated as '*nothing or no-one is going to stop me doing my "job".*' And that job is twenty-four hours a day, seven days a week.

Her 'job' is simply to look after animals – welcome to the world of Princess Elisabeth de Croÿ!

The Princess, the Hippo and other Exotic Creatures: as told by Tim Phillips

For two decades, mine and Elisabeth's paths have frequently crossed, often in extraordinary circumstances – flying in from Greece on board a shaking Ukrainian turboprop freighter with some sixty rescued dogs; in the street markets of Bali, or trying to save a hippo from a French circus. At some stage she became not just another animal protection colleague but a friend and co-conspirator investigating animal suffering, providing information, even pretending to be a French zoo on my behalf in search of an abused circus elephant that had disappeared.

One must set aside any thoughts here of Elisabeth as the aristocrat indulging in animal welfare with a shelter as a compassionate accessory. The first sight of Elisabeth at *Refuge de Thiernay*, looking somewhat grubby in rubber boots with a noisy gaggle of dogs at her heels, turns that image on its head. Although Elisabeth would sweep into our London offices or to receptions and publicity events, glamorous and looking every bit the princess, it is amongst the chasing, happy dogs of the Refuge that she shines. Here she would always be surrounded most closely by the outcasts – the damaged, the odd little dogs that would not find homes: some with misshapen jaws, others with poking out tongues, or missing legs.

We once drove up to her old home, a classic imposing French château. This is what Elisabeth surrendered, for life with a remarkable bunch of yelping and barking misfits.

This is also the humorous and blunt princess. For a film on neutering and shelter operation, I needed to film people touring the shelter looking for dogs to adopt. Elisabeth was pointing out animals, speaking to the potential adopters and also, in a surreal David Attenborough-type way would provide occasional commentary to camera not on the animals, but of the prospective adopters who had incurred her disdain. She turned once and remarked loudly: '*This is*

232

an incredibly stupid person,' pausing and adding with a dismissive gesture *'don't worry they can't understand English.'*

On another occasion our paths crossed in exotic Bali, working with Joy on behalf of WSPA, Elisabeth as an ambassador and myself filming spaying and neutering cats and dogs. We spent dinner in a light-hearted discussion on monarchy: a rare opportunity to have such a chat with a princess! We drifted to the value the British monarchy has to tourism and I remarked that although Alton Towers and Madame Tussauds attracted more visitors than the Queen, I wasn't convinced that they should be given constitutional powers. Elisabeth laughed uproariously. The next day we toured the sad scenes of the animal markets together.

When I was producing the *Refuge de Thiernay* magazine, she would arrive in London with carrier bags of the content for the magazine-to-be. Hundreds of pieces of paper, scraps held together by paper clips, copious handwritten notes. Stories that had to be included for the sake of the animals – their stories had to be told, and others had to be saved and homed. We would have twenty-four pages to fill, about seventy pages of copy, and about twenty-four hours to do it. Older readers will sigh and recall putting together publications like that and the good old days before the personal computer, let alone desktop publishing. But this was 1999. The Refuge was a little behind on the current technology. For our first magazine we featured on the cover, Julius, a delightful scruffy little rescued Yorkshire terrier who had been abused, leaving him with virtually no fur on his back. The half-bald little dog was homed almost immediately.

I suspect it was Julius getting a new life that convinced Elisabeth to keep the magazine going, rather than any public relations or other image value that might otherwise arise from the magazine.

In 1998 ADI concluded the biggest investigation of animal circuses the world has ever seen. ADI Field Officers worked deep undercover inside the circus industry for two years secretly filming, taking photographs, and documenting working practices in detail in most of the UK travelling circuses and training centres and two circuses touring Europe. When the investigation broke, it hit the headlines all over the world; the British animal circus industry collapsed with half the UK's animal circuses closing within six months of the exposé.

The Stop Circus Suffering campaign became a global cause with local and national prohibitions springing up all over the world. Today ADI is working globally, including with Elisabeth in France, to end the abuse of circus animals.

She has always been a huge supporter of this, with a desperate desire to bring people face to face with the cruelty around them; always eager to put disturbing images in her magazine, especially of things she has witnessed herself: '*We must show people the cruelty, show the truth.*'

When we once arrived for a surprise birthday party for her, I think that Elisabeth was just as pleased that we had stopped off on the drive to Nevers to photograph pâté de foie gras production in central France for a campaign: '*Excellent, I once ate that cruel stuff when I did not know how it was made.*'

She has become a regular source of information for us and was always ready to assist. Mary Chipperfield's cousin, Dicky Chipperfield, ran for decades Europe's biggest supplier of performing lions and tigers. I worked undercover at his training facility, alongside another of our ADI Field Officers, feeding and cleaning out the animals. Here these magnificent animals lived in shipping containers and would be whipped and hit or poked with metal bars if they did not do as they were told. It was a wretched place! Once the ADI video hit British TV screens the business collapsed and Chipperfield Enterprises closed their breeding and training centre.

Dicky Chipperfield disappeared until we received a tip-off that he had moved to France and was training lions and tigers with Circus Jean Richard Pinder. As with any French circuses we are tracking, I asked Elisabeth to call various locations as a supposed circus enthusiast and provide volunteers as scouts. We tracked him down and an ADI Field Officer was despatched to secure video footage.

Elisabeth is always eager to investigate and expose animal suffering. I believe she would have loved to have captured on video the events of her youth that shaped her compassion for animals.

In Bali we visited a man who had orang-utans, lions and crocodiles in his yard in tiny, miserable cages. The poor crocodile was living in little more than a coffin, which Elisabeth sat down on at one point, before we realised it contained a living animal. We visited the pet markets where the most beautiful birds, cats, monkeys, and reptiles had been torn from their natural homes to become ornaments for people. Inside a monkey dealer's tent, we found 100 cynomolgus macaques, mostly infants. Many had chains around their necks, lined in rows; our close relatives from the animal kingdom enslaved.

Of course, we were decidedly not undercover – the Englishman and the French princess in the hot, noisy, Balinese street market, although we didn't look like obvious animal protectionists either. But perhaps this was the principle of dazzle camouflage, or hiding in plain sight. As I quietly went about getting as much film and photographs as possible before I was stopped, I heard Elisabeth suddenly embark on a preposterous story of her desire to purchase an orang-utan. I glanced back keeping the camera rolling on the monkeys to see that this included a certain amount of impersonation of an orang-utan, complete with flailing arms! As Elisabeth twittered, I filmed. One of the workers was annoyed with a baby monkey. He picked up a file and hit the animal across the face. It fell off the crate it was chained to, swung by the neck briefly and then climbed back up. I walked around and the little monkey reached up and held my finger; there was a cut above one eye where the file had hit. I fired a photograph one-handed which subsequently appeared full page in the ADI My Mate's a Primate report.

Our toughest challenge was in 2004 when, with Elisabeth we were briefly the owners of a rescued hippo. Several circuses still tour Europe with hippos – although it is hard to imagine a species less suited to such a life. This particular animal lived alone in 20 litres of excrement-contaminated water in a wagon with Circus Zavatta as they toured France. A case was brought against the circus by a collection of French organisations, *Défense et Protection des Animaux, Assistance aux Animaux, One Voice, Ligue de Défense des Droits des Animaux, Fondation Brigitte Bardot.* ADI was called in to secure a home and relocate the animal. This was a male hippo – probably the hardest animal to rehome in the world. Generally, zoos only want females to breed; the huge, potentially very dangerous males are unwanted. I even travelled as far afield as a meeting with Detroit Zoo while searching for a home for this animal.

We headed to court and the French judge ordered that the hippo be taken from the circus and placed in the care of ADI. Briefly, there was the vague possibility that a hippo would join the Thiernay menagerie as we prepared to move him to a more permanent holding facility. But within days, by a cruel twist of fate, the decision was nullified when it was announced that the offences would be covered by a general amnesty for convicts, linked to the recent presidential election! The hippo went back to the circus and other attempts to save him failed.

It is a poignant reminder of how fragile the protection of animals so often is. The sad story of the hippo reminds us that often we appear to be tilting at windmills, yet if we don't take on the challenges we might lose, then we will never change the world for animals, and that's what makes the victories so important. I know Elisabeth shares that view.

Each time we speak, like many others, Elisabeth has something else she would like investigated. She had toured South America and urged: 'You must look into this zoo in Iquitos Peru.' Iquitos is deep in Peru in the Amazon basin, and the largest city in the world that cannot be reached by road. You fly in or go by boat up the Amazon. Hardly somewhere we would be passing!

Yet about a year later I had a team of Field Officers working undercover in South America inside the circus industry. In a thirty-month project we travelled with circuses through Colombia, Bolivia, Ecuador, and Peru catching shocking abuse and violence on film. And we were waiting in Iquitos as a boat laden with exotic animals chugged up the Amazon to perform there. The ADI Field Officers took time to head to that zoo with its performing animal show, and filmed a man tormenting a monkey and jaguar, even forcing the screaming monkey's head into his mouth.

The scenes from this investigation revealed terrible suffering and had an enormous impact as they were repeatedly screened on television in Peru, Colombia, Bolivia, and Ecuador. People began boycotting the cruel travelling circuses and cities and municipalities banned them.

As I write this in 2009, legislation to prohibit animal circuses is before the parliaments of Colombia, Bolivia, Peru and, following another ADI investigation there, Brazil. The Peruvian legislation which was launched at the Congress a year after the investigation by ADI recently passed the committee stage. I hope that by the time this is published we will have a law in Peru that ends the abuse of animals for entertainment, and perhaps that squalid zoo that Elisabeth stumbled on will be closed.

The Birth of ACTAsia: as told by Pei-Feng Su

ACTAsia for Animals represents Action-Compassion-Together and we believe that by working together with local animal protection groups, we can create a more compassionate world for animals. These three words, action, compassion, together, also characterise Princess Elisabeth. We know her as a woman of action, of compassion, who cooperates with and assists like-minded people for the benefit of humans and animals. We are indeed amongst the lucky ones who can count on her continued help and are fortunate not to reside at the 'other end', with her as a fierce opponent.

Our history with Princess Elisabeth goes back fifteen years, to 1994, when she lent her well-known name and presence to a symposium initiated to promote draft animal welfare regulations in Taiwan. This symposium was organised by the first animal welfare organisation in Taiwan, LCA, and at the time Wu Hung and I were the two key members of LCA staff, responsible for organising campaigns.

Some fifteen years ago, 'animal welfare' was unknown terminology for the majority of Taiwanese people. They understood the words 'animal' and 'welfare' individually, but the two words together made no sense in our culture, so working in animal welfare was an extremely difficult and frustrating job and still remains so today in many Asian countries. Some fifteen years ago the media in western countries described Taiwan as 'hell on earth for stray dogs'. Dogs were simply everywhere and lived a miserable, persecuted life on the street, in parks and in schoolyards as the Taiwanese government at the time used only 'catch and kill' methods in their attempts to solve the problem.

I remember that when Princess Elisabeth's visit to Taiwan was confirmed, all of the LCA staff including myself and over 100 volunteers were so excited because we were going to meet a real, live princess who was going to speak to our country on behalf of animals. Taiwan is a very young country and we had no experience of a monarchy so to be able to meet a princess from a European castle was like a fairy-tale for us. We pictured her as a very young lady with blonde hair – either looking like Princess Diana from the UK or one of the princesses from Disney World.

When we received the photos of Princess Elisabeth before her visit to Taiwan, I felt somewhat alarmed and confused. Although she was indeed a glamorous lady, she was a mature person and a brunette, not young and blonde like the image we had 'sold' to the media who were all eagerly waiting to be amongst the first to interview her. I remember a team of us at the office looking at the photographs of Elisabeth, racking our brains trying to come up with an alternative selling point for the media. We were so naïve!

However, her several visits to Taiwan were a great success in promoting animal welfare to the public and were the catalyst for government action; also the media loved her as she generously gave unlimited time to answer their endless questions. Since those days, Princess Elisabeth has keenly followed animal welfare issues in Asia and is most supportive of work being done for animals by the fledgling groups. She often says that Asia is in her heart and Taiwan will always be a special place for her as it opened her eyes to another world.

By 1996 I was disillusioned with 'firefighting' in Taiwan. As a young woman without an animal science degree, higher education or practical 'hands-on' experience my credibility was often questioned, so I decided to travel to western countries to study animal welfare. During this period, Princess Elisabeth provided me with moral guidance and support through her extensive network of contacts and resources. Eventually I gained my Master's degree in the UK (focusing on the animal rights movement) and although I no longer live in Taiwan, I continue to help my Asian colleagues to speak up for animals. So it was a natural progression in 2006 when together with Deepashree Balaram from India, we set up ACTAsia to develop professional animal protectionists in Asia.

Princess Elisabeth was one of the first people to support the birth of ACTAsia, also our first workshop in China. As a start-up group, we didn't even have the funds to cover my air fare but Princess

Elisabeth found a sponsor for us which enabled me to hold a series of workshops in three Chinese cities, attended by almost 200 participants. In 2009 we held our fourth annual workshop for training animal protection groups, but without her initial belief in ACTAsia and her valued support, this would not have been possible.

A Chinese proverb says: 'Every journey begins with a first step.' We still have many steps to take, but we are so thankful that Princess Elisabeth de Croÿ walked the first steps with us and her memory will inspire ACTAsia on our journey to make a better world for animals.

Epilogue

Dr Andrew Rowan, President and Chief Executive Officer, Humane Society International, Humane Society of the United States of America

In over 30 years working in animal protection, I have been fortunate to meet many wonderful people who have devoted their lives to animals but this is not the way animal activities are usually viewed by the rest of the public. It is not that rare for those of us who work in the animal protection movement to receive remarks, both explicit and implicit, that people who love animals do not get along with other people. While it is true that there are some who fit such a characterisation, as a generalisation, the description is totally wrong.

This was clearly demonstrated by a study by one of the first students to graduate from the Tufts Master of Science in Animals and Public Policy. All the Master's students were, at that time, required to undertake a 6–9 month thesis project to graduate and this student chose to analyse data collected by the National Opinion Research Center (NORC) in the United States.

NORC conducts annual surveys of the American public asking the sample a battery of questions on a large variety of topics. Three of the questions/statements can be used to segregate the sample into an 'animal loving' segment (about 11–12 per cent of the total if I remember accurately) and an 'animal using' segment (a little less than 10 per cent). The three questions/statements were:

1) Animals have rights
2) It is acceptable to test cosmetics on animals
3) Do you hunt animals?

241

Those who strongly agreed with (1), strongly disagreed with (2) and answered 'no' to (3) were identified as 'animal lovers'; while those with the opposing pattern of responses were identified as 'animal users'. These two samples could then be examined to identify how they responded to a range of other questions about political affiliation, attitudes to the environment, gay, children's and women's issues, and the like.

The 'animal lovers' turned out to be politically liberal. They tended to be very tolerant of alternative lifestyles and supporters of environmental, children's and women's causes while the 'animal users' were politically conservative and relatively intolerant.

Princess Elisabeth was definitely an 'animal lover' and she exemplified the type of people described in the study and gave the lie to the common stereotype of an animal activist as a people hater. She was a wonderful example of tolerance, passion and compassion. The preceding pages describe what she did for animals over a long and successful life and also provide the reader with a far better window into her motives and interests than I am able to do in this brief epilogue.

For my part, I regret that our paths first crossed relatively late in both our careers (in the late 1990s) but I consider myself blessed to have come to know Princess Elisabeth and to have been able to have joined the legion of her admirers. She loved animals, people and life (not necessarily in that order) and was a wonderful example to the rest of us on how to live life to the full (although she was always fretting about the lack of time she had to complete the tasks before her) and how to comport oneself as an animal activist.

Towards the end of her life, Humane Society International gave her a Lifetime Achievement Award. She honoured us by accepting it and her presence at these gatherings of international animal advocates was an enriching and rewarding experience for all who participated.

Thank you Elisabeth for being you and for being truly present in the lives of so many animals and people!

Nothing is more powerful than an individual acting out of his conscience, thus helping to bring the collective conscience to life.

Norman Cousins

242

Bibliography

Chapters 1 and 2

de Croÿ, Princess Marie, *War Memories* (London: Macmillan and Co. Ltd, 1932)
Martin, Georges, *Histoire et Généalogie de la Maison de Croÿ* (HGMC, 2001)
de Croÿ, Princess Marie-Dorothée, *Le Dame de Valotte* (1996)
Mitchell, Cherry, *The House of Croÿ* (unpublished document 2008)
Mitchell, Cherry, *The Nurse and the Nobility* (unpublished document 2008)

Chapter 3

'Farouk of Egypt Biography', in *Biographybase*. (Article licensed under GNU Free Documentation Licence, using material from Wikipedia article *Farouk of Egypt* 24/07/08)
Robins, Natalie and Aronson, Steven M.L., *Savage Grace* (UK: Gollancz Publishers, 1985)
'Africa mourns Senegal's Senghor' (BBC News website 2001, retrieved 10/09/2008)
A King's Story. The Memoirs of H.R.H. The Duke of Windsor KG. 1953. Published by The Reprint Society Ltd, by arrangement with Messrs Cassell and Co. Ltd in 1953

Chapter 4

de Croÿ, Princess Elisabeth, *Diaries, Algerian War of Independence. 1956* (unpublished)
Schmidl, Erwin A. & Ritter, László, 'The Hungarian Revolution 1956', Osprey Publishing. 2006
Hutt, Charles R. & Lee, William, H.K., '1962 Qazvin (Iran) Earthquake Archive'. Incorporated Research Institutions for Seismology (IRIS) 2004.
de Croÿ, Princess Elisabeth, *Diaries, Nigerian conflict in Biafra 1969* (unpublished)
Philips, Barnaby, *Biafra: Thirty Years on* (BBC News website 2000, retrieved 12/09/08)

Chapter 5

De Wiart, Belgian Minister of Justice, 'The Flooding of the Yser', *Source Records of the Great War, Vol. II* Ed. Charles F. Horne (National Alumni 1923)

Chapter 6

'European Seal Import ban a step closer after crucial EU vote 2 March 2009'. (International Fund for Animal Welfare [IFAW] website)
European Parliament EP NEWS (4–8 July 1988). ISSN – 0250 – 5754 – EP News UK

Chapter 7

Ivanova, Dr O., *Letter from, Cherihiv Region Children's Hospital, Ministry of Health of Ukraine to Princess de Croÿ* (dated 22/07/99)
The Chernobyl Disaster – 20 years on (BBC News Channel 12/06/07)
Furlaud, Alice, A Royal Way with Wayward Animals, *International Herald Tribune*, June 9th 1988, New York Times Service

Chapter 8

Libearty News Issue No. 9 (World Society for the Protection of Animals, January 1995)
Elpida, The Magazine of the Greek Animal Welfare Fund. Issue 3. (1996/7 pages 11–19)

Chapter 9

Extraits du Journal de l'Agriculture du Département de la Nièvre de 1842 (Les Archives Départementales de la Nièvre, pages 298–305)
Kieffer Jean-Pierre, President de l'OABA, 'Jacqueline Gilardoni: Une grande protectrice des animaux', *History section* (l'OABA website)
Information relating to the court action against the Chipperfield family supplied by Animal Defenders International (ADI). Millbank Tower, London SW1P 4QP
My Mate's a Primate (Animal Defenders International 2005. ISBN 0 905225 16 3)

Chapter 10

Goodall, Jane quoted in *AWI Animal Welfare Institute quarterly magazine* (winter 2003)
'Mother Teresa, Biography', in *Nobel Lectures, Peace 1971–1980*, Editor-in-charge Tore Frangsmyr, Editor Irwin Abrams (Singapore, World Scientific Publishing Co., 1997)

Chapter 11

CNPA Conseil National de la Protection Animale (Promotional leaflet 2008)

Chapter 12

Ross, Audrey Burns, *The Relaxation Letters: insights from the famous on life, love and well-being* (Aquarian Press, 1993. ISBN–13: 978–1855383715)

Organisations

ACTAsia for Animals, PO Box 1264, High Wycombe, HP10 8WL, UK

Alliance for Rabies Control (ARC), Balfour and Manson Solicitors, 54–66 Frederick Street, Edinburgh, EH2 1LS, UK

American Society for the Prevention Of Cruelty To Animals (ASPCA), 424 East 92nd Street, New York, NY 10128–6804, USA

Animal Defenders International (ADI), Millbank Tower, Millbank, London SW1P 4QP, UK

Asociación Cubana Para La Proteccion De Animales Y Plantas (ANIPLANT), Calle I-No. 502 entre 23 y 25, Apartado 103, Vedado, CP 10400, Ciudad de la Habana, Cuba

Asociación Humanitaria San Francisco de Asis, c/o/Mr J.E.Leigh, Avenida Loreto 830, Piura, Peru

Chernihiv Region Children's Hospital, vul. Pyrohova 16, Chernihiv, Ukraine

Conseil National de la Protection Animale (CNPA), 10 Place Leon-Blum, F–75011, Paris, France

Compassion In World Farming (CIWF), Second Floor, River Court, Mill Lane, Godalming, Surrey, GU7 1EZ, UK

Compassion Unlimited Plus Action (CUPA), 257, 1st Cross H.A.L. 2nd stage, Indiranagar, Bangalore, 560038, India

Défense et Protection des Animaux (DPA), *Refuge de Thiernay*, La Fermeté, F–58160, Imphy, France

Dogs Trust, 17 Wakley Street, London, EC1V 7RQ, UK

Environment and Animal Society of Taiwan (EAST), No. 137 Lane 304, Sec. 3, Hsin Lung Road, Taipei 116, Taiwan

Eurogroup for Animals, 6, Rue des Patriotes, 1000, Brussels, Belgium

Fondation Assistance Aux Animaux, 23 Avenue de la Republique, 75011 Paris, France

Friends of the Earth, 26–28 Underwood Street, London N1 7JQ, UK

Greek Animal Welfare Fund (GAWF), First Floor, 51 Borough High Street, London, SE1 1NB, UK

Greyhounds in Nood Belgium (GINB), Florastraat 1, 9840 De Pinte, Belgium

Guide Dogs for the Blind Association, Burghfield Common, Reading, RG7 3YG, UK

Help In Suffering (HIS), Maharani Farm, Durgapura, Jaipur, Rajasthan 302 018, India

Humane Society of the United States (HSUS)/Humane Society International, 2100 L Street NW Washington, DC, 20037, USA

International Fund for Animal Welfare (IFAW), 89, Albert Embankment, London SE1 7UD, UK

Internat Velyki Mezhyitichi Orphanage, Koretskyi Region, Rivne Oblast, 34 725 Ukraine

Irish Society for the Prevention of Cruelty to Animals (ISPCA), National Animal Centre, Derrylogher Lodge, Keenagh, Co. Longford, Ireland

Kiev SPA-SOS, 01054 Kyiv, Dmytriwska 17-a, ap.44, Ukraine

Life Conservationist Association (LCA), No. 16, Alley 5, Lane 289, Chuang-Ching Ro, Taipei 110, Taiwan

Massachusetts Society for the Prevention of Cruelty to Animals (MSPCA), 350 S Huntington Ave, Boston, MA 02130, USA

Nadace Na ochranu zvírat (The Animal Protection Trust), Pacovska 31, 140 00 Prague 4, Czech Republic

Mother Teresa Centre, 524 West Calle Primera, Suite No.1005N, San Ysidro, CA 92173, USA

Naturewatch, 14 Hewlett Road, Cheltenham, Gloucestershire, GL52 6AA, UK

Oeuvre d'Assistance Aux Bêtes d'Abattoirs (OABA), Maison des Vétérinaires, 10, Place Léon Blum F75011 Paris, France

Polish Society for the Protection of Animals (OTOZ), Ul. Imbirowa 3d/36, 81–591, Gdynia, Poland

Protection Mondiale des Animaux de Ferme (PMAF), 8 ter en Chandellerue, BP 80242, 57006 Metz cedex 1, France

Royal Society for the Prevention of Cruelty to Animals (RSPCA), Wilberforce Way, Southwater, Horsham, West Sussex, RH13 9RS, UK

Sebakwe Black Rhino Trust, Manor Farm, Ascott-under-Wychwood, Oxon, OX7 6AL, UK

SNIP International, Preddanak, Loe Bar Road, Porthleven, Helston, Cornwall, TR13 9ET, UK

Stichting AAP, P.O. Box 50313, 1305 AH Almere, Holland

Swiss Red Cross, Schweizerisches Rotes Kreuz, Rainmattstrass 10, CH–3001, Bern, Switzerland

The Animal Rescue Charity (ARC), Foxdells Sanctuary, Foxdells Lane, Rye Street, Bishop's Stortford, Herts, CM23 2JG, UK

The Mayhew Animal Home, Trenmar Gardens, Kensal Green, London NW10 6BJ, UK

The United Nations Children's Fund (UNICEF), UNICEF House, 30a Great Sutton Street, London EC1V ODU, UK.

Tierhilfswerk Austria, Capistrangasse 3/4, A–1060, Vienna, Austria

Towarzystwo Opieki nad Zwierzetami w Polsce (TOZ), Zarzad Glówny w Warszawie, ul. Noakowskiego 4, 00–666, Warszawa, Poland

Turkiye Hayvanlari Koruma Dernegi (THKD), Matbaaci Osmanbey Sk. No: 30, Sisli, Istanbul, Turkey

Union De Amigos De Los Animales (UAA), Almirante Riveros 030-A Providencia, Casilla 2127, Santiago, Chile

Wood Green Animal Shelters (WGAS), Kings Bush Farm, London Road, Godmanchester, Cambridgeshire, PE29 2NH, UK

World Society for the Protection of Animals (WSPA), 5th Floor, 222 Grays Inn Road, London WC1X 8HB

Yayasan Yudisthira Swarga, Jl Tukad Balian 170, Renon, Denpasar, Bali, 80226, Indonesia

Index

Page references in *italic* indicate photographs.